The Works of
John Clare

with an Introduction by John Goodridge,
and Bibliography

Wordsworth Poetry Library

This edition published 1995 by Wordsworth Editions Ltd,
Cumberland House, Crib Street, Ware, Hertfordshire SG12 9ET.

ISBN 1-85326-434-2

Printed and bound in Denmark by Nørhaven.

The paper in this book is produced from pure wood
pulp, without the use of chlorine or any other substance
harmful to the environment. The energy used in its
production consists almost entirely of hydroelectricity
and heat generated from waste materials, thereby
conserving fossil fuels and contributing little to the
greenhouse effect.

CONTENTS

INTRODUCTION ix

POEMS OF RURAL LIFE:
Address to Plenty 1
Approach of Spring 9
Summer. 9
Noon 10
Falling Leaves 12
To my Oaten Reed 13

THE VILLAGE MINSTREL:
William and Robin 14
The Cross Roads 17
Recollections after an Evening Walk . . . 26
Cowper Green. 28
The Wood-Cutter's Night Song 34
A Pastoral 35
The Request 37
Song 38
Song 39
Song 40
Impromptu 41
To the Butterfly 41
To the Rural Muse 43
To Autumn 44
In Hilly-Wood. 45
Morning 45
To an Hour-Glass 46
A Cottage 46
Solitude. 47
Ballad 56

CONTENTS

THE SHEPHERD'S CALENDAR:

    February 57
    April 62
    July 66
    November 70
    Life, Death, and Eternity 73

THE RURAL MUSE:

    Autumn. 74
    Summer Images 78
    Insects 85
    Sudden Shower 86
    Beans in Blossom 86
    Evening Primrose 87
    The Shepherd's Tree. 87
    Nutting 88
    Death of a Beauty 88
    Decay 89

MANUSCRIPT BOOK:

    The Flitting 89
    Remembrances 96
    Expectations 100
    The Toper's Rant 102
    The Cottager 103
    Shadows of Taste 106
    The Progress of Rhyme 111
    Pleasures of Fancy 121
    To Charles Lamb 122
    Swordy Well 122
    The Instinct of Hope 123
    Providence 123
    Flattery 124
    Nature 124
    Home Pictures in May 125
    Summer Evening 125
    Autumn 126

CONTENTS

Emmonsail's Heath in Winter 126
Greensward 127
The Wheat Ripening 127
The Meadow Hay 128
The Sallow 128
The Firetail's Nest 129
The Fear of Flowers 129
Wild Bees 130
To Content 131

POEMS IN THE MANNER OF OLDER POETS:
Farewell and Defiance to Love 133
To John Milton 135
The Vanities of Life 138
On Death 142

ASYLUM POEMS:
Left alone 145
My Early Home 145
Home Yearnings 146
Mary Bateman 148
Mary 148
The Tell-tale Flowers 150
I'll dream upon the days to come 153
Birds, why are ye silent? 154
The Invitation 155
The Lover's Invitation 156
The Morning Walk 157
The March Nosegay 158
Bonny Mary O! 159
Where she told her love 160
The face I love so dearly 161
Evening 162
Evening 162
Autumn 163
The Beanfield 164
The Swallow 164

viii CONTENTS

To my Wife 164
Maid of the Wilderness 166
Bonnie Lassie O! 167
Young Jennie 168
Adieu 169
My True Love is a Sailor 170
The Gipsy Lass 171
Clock-a-clay 172
Little Trotty Wagtail 173
Graves of Infants 173
The Dying Child 174
Love lies beyond the Tomb 175
I am! 176

GLOSSARY 177

INTRODUCTION

CLARE'S is an extraordinary story. Now regarded by many as the finest and most subtly convincing of the English rural poets, Clare was born into a village community which had little time for poetry, and he was essentially self-taught, writing his first verses in secret in his teens. He was 'discovered' by a London publisher and achieved celebrity as the latest in a long line of 'peasant poets', a kind of novelty-act. This kind of fame was fleeting as well as limiting, and although he would continue to write poetry throughout his life, Clare's material circumstances deteriorated, his world becoming ever darker. Incredibly and tragically, he spent the last twenty-three years of his life locked away in a lunatic asylum, apparently forgotten. As Clare himself put it in a famous lament, 'I Am' (the final poem in the present selection):

> I am! yet what I am none cares or knows,
> My friends forsake me like a memory lost;
> I am the self-consumer of my woes...

John Clare was born at Helpston, Northampton-shire, a 'gloomy village' on the edge of the Cambridgeshire fens, on 13 July 1793. His father Parker, the illegitimate son of an itinerant Scottish schoolmaster, was an agricultural labourer, famed locally for his prowess at wrestling, geniality over a drinking horn, and ballad-singing. Clare's mother Ann, 'gypsy-like in her appearance', was the daughter of a shepherd and the sister of a drover. Clare's twin sister Bessy died in infancy, contributing perhaps to his later sense of estrangement and loss.

As a child he went threshing corn in winter, and in summer was given field-work. He enjoyed working with the old women who told him stories to pass the time, and was especially fond of 'Granny Bains', a cattle herder who taught him songs and ballads. When he could be spared from work he attended a dame school in the village. Later he went to a vestry school at Glinton church, where he met Mary Joyce, whom he would love and lose, and with whom he would become obsessed. Clare was encouraged by his teachers, despite village hostility to book-learning and reading ('a sure indication of laziness'), and his parents also encouraged him to persist in acquiring knowledge. Clare's formal education ended when he was eleven, but he continued to educate himself. He also began to write poetry. From his earliest days Clare loved songs, stories, and the popular printed tales and ballads that were hawked around the villages 'a penny a sheet', often illustrated with woodcuts. At thirteen he discovered another kind of poetry, in James Thomson's rural epic, *The Seasons*. This was a revelation to Clare, and led him directly to the first poem he wrote down, 'The Evening Walk'.

A number of possible jobs and apprenticeships were considered and rejected. After an unhappy few months as a ploughboy, Clare worked for a year at the Bluebell Inn in Helpston, next door to his parent's cottage. This gave him leisure to compose poetry. It also meant regular journeys to the flour mill at Maxey, walking at night past notoriously haunted spots. These journeys terrified Clare, who was deeply sensitive to such things, and his common habit of talking aloud, reciting verses and telling himself stories, was among other things a way of keeping the spirit world at bay. Clare worked as a gardener at Burghley House, where he learned 'irregular habbits'. In 1812 he joined the militia, distinguishing himself by seizing a bullying corporal by the throat and hurling him to the ground. Clare appears to have worked at Burghley again in 1816-17. His relationship with his childhood sweetheart Mary Joyce suddenly ended in 1816, almost certainly under pressure from her father, who would see little prospect of a suitable marriage for his daughter in this dreamy village boy. Clare was unhappy at Burghley, and in 1817 (when his father, now crippled by rheumatism, was forced to go to the Parish for help) he again left home to earn money. This time he went lime-burning at Great Casterton, north of Stamford. In the nearby village of Tickencote he and his fellow workers would drink on Sundays, and here Clare first saw Martha Turner, the daughter of a farmer from nearby Walkherd. They were married in early 1820, when Patty (as Martha was usually called) was, as Clare tactfully puts it, 'in a situation that marriage only could remedy'.

By 1817-18 Clare had amassed enough poetry to consider possible publication. He had been hanging round the bookshops of Stamford and Market Deeping – the nearest centres of literary activity – at every opportunity for a number of years. Now he got as far as printing a prospectus for publishing his poetry by subscription. The scheme collapsed when Clare couldn't pay the bill for the prospectuses, and only a few people ever subscribed. But then in 1819 Edward Drury, the young, ambitious cousin of Keats' publisher John Taylor, purchased the main bookshop at Stamford, and Clare's fate was decided. Along with the shop Drury took over Clare's stationery debts, and he was astute enough to write these off by way of buying into this interesting rustic poet. John Taylor was duly summoned from London to meet Clare, and thus *Poems Descriptive of Rural Life and Scenery by John Clare, a Northamptonshire Peasant* was published by Taylor and Hessey of Fleet Street and Edward Drury of Stamford, on 16 January 1820. Within a year it was well into its fourth edition. 1820 was Clare's *annus mirabilis*: annuities were settled on him by the good and the great, he visited London (the first of four visits) and had his portrait painted by William Hilton, RA. As a literary celebrity he acquired patrons and literary friends. His first child was born.

The sunshine, however, would not last long. His novelty value waned, and each successive volume sold fewer copies, while the financial pressure to care for ageing parents and a growing family steadily increased. Clare never entirely escaped from farm labour, even at the height of his fame. It is extraordinary that despite these pressures, he managed to produce poetry and prose of such high quality, and so prolifically, throughout the 1820s. But his masterpiece, *The Shepherd's Calendar*, had its publication held back some three years and half its lines removed. And *The Midsummer Cushion*, Clare's outstanding selection of his best poetry, put together in 1831-2, was published only in a greatly reduced form and after yet another long delay. Clare must have felt daunted as he moved into his middle years.

In 1832 his patrons devised what they imagined to be a solution to his problems: they found him a cottage and bit of land in the village of Northborough. His patron Eliza Emmerson dubbed him 'Farmer John' and sent him ten pounds to buy a cow. But Northborough was no solution. Clare could not go back to farming; much less could he abandon his poetic ambitions. He had invested far too much in them even to consider it. And although Northborough was only a few miles north-east of Helpston, for an intensely-rooted man like Clare it might just as well have been on the moon. He felt exiled. He had always been prone to depression and anxiety. Now depression began to turn to withdrawal, and withdrawal to delusion.

In 1837 his patrons had him removed to Matthew Allen's asylum at High Beach in Epping Forest. This was a fairly progressive establishment, and Clare regained his physical, if not his mental health. Four years later he walked home. His extraordinary account of the eighty-mile journey is one of the most moving things he ever wrote. Cold, hungry, exhausted, hallucinating, eating grass to fill his belly, he was determined to get back to his 'wife' Mary Joyce. (Mary was not of course his wife, and had died in 1838, which Clare adamantly refused to believe.) He remained at Northborough, 'homeless at home', for a few months. Then on 29 December 1841 he was forcibly and permanently removed to the Northampton General Lunatic

Asylum. The certification document says among other things that Clare was suffering from hereditary insanity and the adverse effect of 'years of addiction to poetical prosings'. This is of course sheerest quackery, though Clare was undeniably ill, and beyond the care of his family. Victorian mental health care served him well in one respect, at least, for the 'moral regime' practised at Northampton fostered therapeutic activities, so that Clare was encouraged to continue writing his poetry for most of the twenty-three years remaining to him. He died of a stroke, late in the afternoon of 20 May, 1864, aged seventy.

Clare has always been appreciated for his lyrical celebration of rural life, written in vivid and accessible poetry. The poignancy of his life has also led to much interest in his visionary asylum verse, and in other areas of his writings relating to his life, such as his fragmentary but exceptionally interesting autobiographical prose writings. Nowadays Clare is appreciated by more readers than ever before, and for a wider range of reasons. He is valued as a lively narrative poet, an interesting if rather sentimental folklorist, an important early recorder of folksong, and a gifted and observant amateur naturalist. Perhaps most interestingly for the modern reader, with our intense consciousness of green issues and the lost rural past, Clare is valued as the verse-spokesman for the villager and the village community. Even more than Wordsworth he is the champion of the local and the particular, the marginalised and the undervalued, both in the human world and in all those fragile and vital areas of nature, threatened then (and now) by human predation and exploitation.

The present edition of Clare reprints the selection made by Arthur Symons in 1908, which has an historical interest in terms of changing perceptions of Clare, and gives a good selection of Clare's lyrical, narrative and visionary verse. Symons left out Clare's more political and satirical poetry, and routinely corrected his spelling and added punctuation, whereas modern editors and critics (see below) tend to prefer Clare uncorrected and unpunctuated, and are more enthusiastic

about his politically outspoken poems. Keen readers will want
to sample both approaches to this most rich and evocative poet.

John Goodridge
The Nottingham Trent University, 1994

FURTHER READING

The Clarendon Press (Oxford English Texts) edition of Clare's poetry, edited
by Eric Robinson and others, is standard. There are also useful selections of
poetry and prose published by Carcanet, Methuen, Oxford, and Penguin.

John Barrell, *The Idea of Landscape and the Sense of Place, 1730-1840: an
approach to the poetry of John Clare* (Cambridge, 1972)

Edward Storey, *A Right to Song: The Life of John Clare* (1982)
John Clare's Autobiographical Writings, ed. Eric Robinson (Oxford, 1983)
The Natural History Prose Writings of John Clare, ed. Margaret Grainger
(Oxford, 1983)
George Deacon, *John Clare and the Folk Tradition* (1983)
The Letters of John Clare, ed. Mark Storey (Oxford, 1985)
John Clare in Context, ed, Hugh Haughton, Adam Phillips and Geoffrey
Summerfield (Cambridge, 1994)

ADDRESS TO PLENTY

IN WINTER

O THOU Bliss! to riches known,
Stranger to the poor alone;
Giving most where none's requir'd,
Leaving none where most's desir'd;
Who, sworn friend to miser, keeps,
Adding to his useless heaps
Gifts on gifts, profusely stor'd,
Till thousands swell the mouldy hoard
While poor, shatter'd Poverty,
To advantage seen in me,
With his rags, his wants, and pain,
Waking pity but in vain,
Bowing, cringing at thy side,
Begs his mite, and is denied.
O, thou Blessing! let not me
Tell, as vain, my wants to thee;
Thou, by name of Plenty stil'd,
Fortune's heir, her favourite child.
'Tis a maxim—hunger feed,
Give the needy when they need;
He, whom all profess to serve,
The same maxim did observe:
Their obedience here, how well,
Modern times will plainly tell.
Hear my wants, nor deem me bold,
Not without occasion told:
Hear one wish; nor fail to give;
Use me well, and bid me live.

'Tis not great, what I solicit;
Was it more, thou couldst not miss it:
Now the cutting Winter's come,
'Tis but just to find a home,
In some shelter, dry and warm,
That will shield me from the storm.
Toiling in the naked fields,
Where no bush a shelter yields,
Needy Labour dithering stands,
Beats and blows his numbing hands;
And upon the crumping snows
Stamps, in vain, to warm his toes.
Leaves are fled, that once had power
To resist a summer shower;
And the wind so piercing blows,
Winnowing small the drifting snows,
The summer shade of loaded bough
Would vainly boast a shelter now:
Piercing snows so searching fall,
They sift a passage through them all.
Though all's vain to keep him warm,
Poverty must brave the storm.
Friendship none, its aid to lend:
Health alone his only friend;
Granting leave to live in pain,
Giving strength to toil in vain;
To be, while winter's horrors last,
The sport of every pelting blast.

Oh, sad sons of Poverty!
Victims doom'd to misery;
Who can paint what pain prevails
O'er that heart which Want assails?
Modest Shame the pain conceals:
No one knows, but he who feels.
O thou charm which Plenty crowns,

Fortune! smile, now Winter frowns:
Cast around a pitying eye;
Feed the hungry, ere they die.
Think, oh! think upon the poor,
Nor against them shut thy door:
Freely let thy bounty flow,
On the sons of Want and Woe.

Hills and dales no more are seen
In their dress of pleasing green;
Summer's robes are all thrown by,
For the clothing of the sky;
Snows on snows in heaps combine,
Hillocks, rais'd as mountains, shine,
And at distance rising proud,
Each appears a fleecy cloud.
Plenty! now thy gifts bestow;
Exit bid to every woe:
Take me in, shut out the blast,
Make the doors and windows fast;
Place me in some corner, where,
Lolling in an elbow chair,
Happy, blest to my desire,
I may find a rouzing fire;
While in chimney-corner nigh,
Coal, or wood, a fresh supply,
Ready stands for laying on,
Soon as t' other's burst and gone.
Now and then, as taste decreed,
In a book a page I'd read;
And, inquiry to amuse,
Peep at something in the news;
See who's married, and who's dead,
And who, though bankrupt, beg their bread:
While on hob, or table nigh,
Just to drink before I'm dry,

A pitcher at my side should stand,
With the barrel nigh at hand,
Always ready as I will'd,
When 'twas empty, to be fill'd;
And, to be possess'd of all,
A corner cupboard in the wall,
With store of victuals lin'd complete,
That when hungry I might eat.
Then would I, in Plenty's lap,
For the first time take a nap;
Falling back in easy lair,
Sweetly slumb'ring in my chair;
With no reflective thoughts to wake
Pains that cause my heart to ache,
Of contracted debts, long made,
In no prospect to be paid;
And, to Want, sad news severe,
Of provisions getting dear:
While the Winter, shocking sight,
Constant freezes day and night,
Deep and deeper falls the snow,
Labour's slack, and wages low.
These, and more, the poor can tell,
Known, alas, by them too well,
Plenty! oh, if blest by thee,
Never more should trouble me.
Hours and weeks will sweetly glide,
Soft and smooth as flows the tide,
Where no stones or choaking grass
Force a curve ere it can pass:
And as happy, and as blest,
As beasts drop them down to rest,
When in pastures, at their will,
They have roam'd and eat their fill;
Soft as nights in summer creep,
So should I then fall asleep;

While sweet visions of delight,
So enchanting to the sight,
Sweetly swimming o'er my eyes,
Would sink me into extacies.
Nor would Pleasure's dreams once more,
As they oft have done before,
Cause be to create a pain,
When I woke, to find them vain :
Bitter past, the present sweet,
Would my happiness complete.
Oh ! how easy should I lie,
With the fire up-blazing high,
(Summer's artificial bloom,)
That like an oven keeps the room,
Or lovely May, as mild and warm :
While, without, the raging storm
Is roaring in the chimney-top,
In no likelihood to drop ;
And the witchen-branches nigh,
O'er my snug box towering high,
That sweet shelter'd stands beneath,
In convulsive eddies wreathe.
Then while, tyrant-like, the storm
Takes delight in doing harm,
Down before him crushing all,
Till his weapons useless fall ;
And as in oppression proud
Peal his howlings long and loud,
While the clouds, with horrid sweep,
Give (as suits a tyrant's trade)
The sun a minute's leave to peep,
To smile upon the ruins made ;
And to make complete the blast,
While the hail comes hard and fast,
Rattling loud against the glass ;
And the snowy sleets, that pass,

Driving up in heaps remain
Close adhering to the pane,
Stop the light, and spread a gloom,
Suiting sleep, around the room:—
Oh, how blest 'mid these alarms,
I should bask in Fortune's arms,
Who, defying every frown,
Hugs me on her downy breast,
Bids my head lie easy down,
And on Winter's ruins rest.
So upon the troubled sea,
Emblematic simile,
Birds are known to sit secure,
While the billows roar and rave,
Slumbering in their safety sure,
Rock'd to sleep upon the wave.
So would I still slumber on,
Till hour-telling clocks had gone,
And, from the contracted day,
One or more had click'd away.
Then with sitting wearied out,
I for change's sake, no doubt,
Just might wish to leave my seat,
And, to exercise my feet,
Make a journey to the door,
Put my nose out, but no more ·
There to village taste agree;
Mark how times are like to be;
How the weather's getting on ;
Peep in ruts where carts have gone ;
Or, by stones, a sturdy stroke,
View the hole the boys have broke,
Crizzling, still inclin'd to freeze ;—
And the rime upon the trees.
Then to pause on ills to come,
Just look upward on the gloom;

See fresh storms approaching fast,
View them busy in the air,
Boiling up the brewing blast,
Still fresh horrors scheming there.
Black and dismal, rising high,
From the north they fright the eye:
Pregnant with a thousand storms,
Huddled in their icy arms,
Heavy hovering as they come,
Some as mountains seem—and some
Jagg'd as craggy rocks appear
Dismally advancing near:
Fancy, at the cumbrous sight,
Chills and shudders with affright,
Fearing lest the air, in vain,
Strive her station to maintain,
And wearied, yielding to the skies,
The world beneath in ruin lies.
So may Fancy think and feign;
Fancy oft imagines vain:
Nature's laws, by wisdom penn'd,
Mortals cannot comprehend;
Power almighty Being gave,
Endless Mercy stoops to save;
Causes, hid from mortals' sight,
Prove 'whatever is, is right.'

Then to look again below,
Labour's former life I'd view,
Who, still beating through the snow,
Spite of storms their toils pursue,
Forc'd out by sad Necessity,
That sad fiend that forces me.
Troubles, then no more my own,
Which I but too long had known,
Might create a care, a pain;

Then I'd seek my joys again:
Pile the fire up, fetch a drink,
Then sit down again and think;
Pause on all my sorrows past,
Think how many a bitter blast,
When it snow'd, and hail'd, and blew,
I have toil'd and batter'd through.
Then to ease reflective pain,
To my sports I'd fall again,
Till the clock had counted ten;
When I'd seek my downy bed,
Easy, happy, and well fed.

Then might peep the morn, in vain,
Through the rimy misted pane;
Then might bawl the restless cock,
And the loud-tongued village clock;
And the flail might lump away,
Waking soon the dreary day.
They should never waken me,
Independent, blest, and free;
Nor, as usual, make me start,
Yawning sigh with heavy heart,
Loth to ope my sleepy eyes,
Weary still, in pain to rise,
With aching bones and heavy head,
Worse than when I went to bed.
With nothing then to raise a sigh,
Oh, how happy should I lie
Till the clock was eight, or more,
Then proceed as heretofore.
Best of blessings! sweetest charm!
Boon these wishes while they're warm;
My fairy visions ne'er despise;
As reason thinks, thou realize:
Depress'd with want and poverty,
I sink, I fall, denied by thee.

APPROACH OF SPRING

SWEET are the omens of approaching Spring
  When gay the elder sprouts her winged leaves;
When tootling robins carol-welcomes sing,
  And sparrows chelp glad tidings from the eaves.
What lovely prospects wait each wakening hour,
  When each new day some novelty displays;
How sweet the sun-beam melts the crocus flower,
  Whose borrow'd pride shines dizen'd in his rays:
Sweet, new-laid hedges flush their tender greens;
Sweet peep the arum-leaves their shelter screens;
  Ah! sweet is all which I'm denied to share:
Want's painful hindrance sticks me to her stall;—
  But still Hope's smiles unpoint the thorns of Care,
Since Heaven's eternal Spring is free for all.

SUMMER

THE oak's slow-opening leaf, of deepening hue,
  Bespeaks the power of Summer once again;
While many a flower unfolds its charms to view,
  To glad the entrance of his sultry reign.
Where peep the gaping speckled cuckoo-flowers,
  Sweet is each rural scene she brings to pass;
Prizes to rambling school-boys' vacant hours,
  Tracking wild searches through the meadow grass:
The meadow-sweet taunts high its showy wreath,
And sweet the quaking-grasses hide beneath.
  Ah, 'barr'd from all that sweetens life below,
Another Summer still my eyes can see
  Freed from the scorn and pilgrimage of woe,
To share the Seasons of Eternity.

NOON

ALL how silent and how still;
Nothing heard but yonder mill:
While the dazzled eye surveys
All around a liquid blaze;
And amid the scorching gleams,
If we earnest look, it seems
As if crooked bits of glass
Seem'd repeatedly to pass.
Oh, for a puffing breeze to blow!
But breezes are all strangers now;
Not a twig is seen to shake,
Nor the smallest bent to quake;
From the river's muddy side
Not a curve is seen to glide;
And no longer on the stream
Watching lies the silver bream,
Forcing, from repeated springs,
'Verges in successive rings.'
Bees are faint, and cease to hum;
Birds are overpower'd and dumb.
Rural voices all are mute,
Tuneless lie the pipe and flute:
Shepherds, with their panting sheep,
In the swaliest corner creep;
And from the tormenting heat
All are wishing to retreat.
Huddled up in grass and flowers,
Mowers wait for cooler hours;
And the cow-boy seeks the sedge,
Ramping in the woodland hedge,
While his cattle o'er the vales
Scamper, with uplifted tails;

Others not so wild and mad,
That can better bear the gad,
Underneath the hedge-row lunge,
Or, if nigh, in waters plunge.
Oh! to see how flowers are took,
How it grieves me when I look:
Ragged-robins, once so pink,
Now are turn'd as black as ink,
And the leaves, being scorch'd so much,
Even crumble at the touch;
Drowking lies the meadow-sweet,
Flopping down beneath one's feet:
While to all the flowers that blow,
If in open air they grow,
Th' injurious deed alike is done
By the hot relentless sun.
E'en the dew is parched up
From the teasel's jointed cup:
O poor birds! where must ye fly,
Now your water-pots are dry?
If ye stay upon the heath,
Ye'll be choak'd and clamm'd to death.
Therefore leave the shadeless goss,
Seek the spring-head lin'd with moss;
There your little feet may stand,
Safely printing on the sand;
While, in full possession, where
Purling eddies ripple clear,
You with ease and plenty blest,
Sip the coolest and the best.
Then away! and wet your throats;
Cheer me with your warbling notes;
'Twill hot noon the more revive;
While I wander to contrive
For myself a place as good,
In the middle of a wood:

There aside some mossy bank,
Where the grass in bunches rank
Lifts its down on spindles high,
Shall be where I'll choose to lie;
Fearless of the things that creep,
There I'll think, and there I'll sleep;
Caring not to stir at all,
Till the dew begins to fall.

FALLING LEAVES

HAIL, falling Leaves! that patter round,
  Admonishers and friends;
Reflection wakens at the sound—
  So, Life, thy pleasure ends.

How frail the bloom, how short the stay,
  That terminates us all!
To-day we flourish green and gay,
  Like leaves to-morrow fall.

Alas! how short is fourscore years,
  Life's utmost stretch,—a span;
And shorter still, when past, appears
  The vain, vain life of man.

These falling leaves once flaunted high,
  O pride! how vain to trust:
Now wither'd on the ground they lie,
  And mingled with the dust.

So Death serves all—and wealth and pride
  Must all their pomp resign;
E'en kings shall lay their crowns aside,
  To mix their dust with mine.

The leaves, how once they cloth'd the trees,
  None's left behind to tell;
The branch is naked to the breeze;
  We know not whence they fell.

A few more years, and I the same
  As they are now, shall be,
With nothing left to tell my name,
  Or answer, 'Who was he?'

Green turf's allow'd forgotten heap
  Is all that I shall have,
Save that the little daisies creep
  To deck my humble grave.

TO MY OATEN REED

THOU Warble wild of rough rude melody!
  How oft I've woo'd thee, often thrown thee by;
In many a doubtful rapture touching thee,
  Waking thy rural notes in many a sigh:
  Fearing the wise, the wealthy, proud and high,
Would scorn as vain thy lowly extasy;
  Deeming presumptuous thy uncultur'd themes.
Thus vainly courting Taste's unblemish'd eye,
  To list a simple Labourer's artless dreams,
  Haply I wander into wide extremes.
But O thou sweet wild-winding rhapsody,
  Thou jingling charm that dost my heart control;
I take thee up to smother many a sigh,
  And lull the throbbings of a woe-worn soul.

WILLIAM AND ROBIN

WILLIAM

When I meet Peggy in my morning walk,
She first salutes the morn, then stays to talk:
The biggest secret she will not refuse,
But freely tells me all the village-news;
And pleas'd am I, can I but haply force
Some new-made tale to lengthen the discourse,
For—O so pleasing is her company,
That hours, like minutes, in her presence fly!
I'm happy then, nor can her absence e'er
Raise in my heart the least distrust or fear.

ROBIN

When Mary meets me I find nought to say,
She hangs her head, I turn another way;
Sometimes (but never till the maid's gone by)
'Good morning!' falters, weaken'd by a sigh;
Confounded I remain, but yet delight
To look back on her till she's out of sight.
Then, then's the time that absence does torment:
I jeer my weakness, painfully repent,
To think how well I might have then confest
That secret love which makes me so distrest:
But, when the maiden's vanish'd for a while,
Recruited hopes my future hours beguile:
I fancy then another time I'll tell,
Which, if not better, will be quite as well;
Thus days, and weeks, and months I've dallied o'er,
And am no nearer than I was before.

WILLIAM

Such ways as these I ever strove to shun,
Nor was I bashful when I first begun:

Freely I offer'd posies to the maid,
Which she as freely with her smiles repaid;
Yet had I been, like you, afraid to own
My love—her kindness had been still unknown.
And, now the maiden's kindness to requite,
I strive to please her morning, noon, and night:
The garland and the wreath for her I bind,
Compos'd of all the fairest I can find;
For her I stop the straggler going astray,
And watch her sheep when she's not in the way;
I fetch them up at night, and shift the pen,
And in the morning let them out again:
For her in harvest when the nuts are brown,
I take my crook to pull the branches down;
And up the trees that dismally hang o'er
The deep black pond, where none durst go before,
I heedless climb, as free from fear as now,
And snatch the clusters from the topmost bough;
Well pleas'd to risk such dangers that can prove
How much her William does his Peggy love.

ROBIN

I search the meadows, and as well as you
I bind up posies, and sweet garlands too;
And if I unawares can hear exprest
What flower she fancies finer than the rest,
Grow where it will, I search the fields about,
And search for 't daily till I find it out;
And when I've found it—oh—what tongue can tell
The fears and doubts which in my bosom swell:
The schemes contriving, and the plans I lay,
How I to her the garland may convey,
Are various indeed;—sometimes I start,
Resolv'd to tell the secret of my heart,
Vowing to make the gather'd garland prove
How much I languish, and how much I love:

But soon resolves and vows allay their heat,
And timid weakness reassumes her seat.
The garland then, which I so painful sought,
Instantly seems as if 'twere good for nought:
'Ah, gaudy thing!' I sigh, 'will Mary wear
Such foolish lumber in her auburn hair?'
Thus doubts and fears each other thought confound,
And, thus perplex'd, I throw it on the ground—
Walk from 't, distrest—in pensive silence mourn,
Then plan a scheme, and back again return:
Once more the garland in my hand I take,
And of the best a smaller posy make,
Resting assur'd that such a nosegay will
To gain her favour prove a better still,
And then my hopeful heart's from grief reviv'd
By this new plan, so seeming well-contriv'd;
So off I go, and gain the spot—ah, then
I sneak along—my heart misgives again,
And as I nearer draw, 'Well now,' thinks I,
'I'll not speak to her, but pass silent by:'
Then from my coat that precious gift I take,
Which I beforehand treasur'd for her sake;
And after all my various scheming so,
The flowers, as worthless, to the ground I throw.
And then, if getting through the hedge-bound plain,
Having no sense to find the same again,
Her little lambkins raise a piteous cry,
Calling for help—whether far off or nigh
It matters not, can I but hear their moan,
(Of her's more tender am I than my own,)
The journey's nought at all, no steps I grudge,
But with great pleasure to their aid I trudge;
Yet this is never to the maiden known,
Nor ever done save only when alone,
Fearing from it that other swains should prove,
Or she herself, the favour to be love.

Though in her absence I so fond appear,
Yet when she 's there I'm careless, as it were;
Nor can I have the face, although my mind
At the same time's most willingly inclin'd,
To do the least kind act at all for her,
Nor join the tale where she does interfere.
If from her looks a smile I e'er obtain,
I feel o'erjoy'd but never smile again;
And when I hear the swains her beauty praise,
And try with artful, fond, alluring ways
To snatch the posy from her swelling breast,
And loose the ribbon round her slender waist,
Then more familiar touch her curling hair,
And praise her beauty as beyond compare;
At this sad pains around my heart will sting,
But I ne'er look, nor tell a single thing.

THE CROSS ROADS;

OR, THE HAYMAKER'S STORY

Stopt by the storm, that long in sullen black
From the south-west stain'd its encroaching track,
Haymakers, hustling from the rain to hide,
Sought the grey willows by the pasture-side;
And there, while big drops bow the grassy stems,
And bleb the withering hay with pearly gems,
Dimple the brook, and patter in the leaves,
The song or tale an hour's restraint relieves.
And while the old dames gossip at their ease,
And pinch the snuff-box empty by degrees,
The young ones join in love's delightful themes,
Truths told by gipsies, and expounded dreams;
And mutter things kept secrets from the rest,
As sweetheart's names, and whom they love the best;

And dazzling ribbons they delight to show,
The last new favours of some 'veigling beau,
Who with such treachery tries their hearts to move,
And, like the highest, bribes the maidens' love.
The old dames, jealous of their whisper'd praise,
Throw in their hints of man's deluding ways;
And one, to give her counsels more effect,
And by example illustrate the fact
Of innocence o'ercome by flattering man,
Thrice tapp'd her box, and pinch'd, and thus began.

'Now wenches listen, and let lovers lie,
Ye'll hear a story ye may profit by;
I'm your age treble, with some oddments to't,
And right from wrong can tell, if ye'll but do't:
Ye need not giggle underneath your hat,
Mine's no joke-matter, let me tell you that;
So keep ye quiet till my story's told,
And don't despise your betters cause they're old.

'That grave ye've heard of, where the four roads
　　　meet,
Where walks the spirit in a winding-sheet,
Oft seen at night, by strangers passing late,
And tarrying neighbours that at market wait,
Stalking along as white as driven snow,
And long as one's shadow when the sun is low;
The girl that's buried there I knew her well,
And her whole history, if ye'll hark, can tell.
Her name was Jane, and neighbour's children we,
And old companions once, as ye may be;
And like to you, on Sundays often stroll'd
To gipsies' camps to have our fortunes told;
And oft, God rest her, in the fortune-book
Which we at hay-time in our pockets took,
Our pins at blindfold on the wheel we stuck,
When hers would always prick the worst of luck

For try, poor thing, as often as she might,
Her point would always on the blank alight;
Which plainly shows the fortune one's to have,
As such like go unwedded to the grave,—
And so it prov'd.—The next succeeding May,
We both to service went from sports and play,
Though in the village still; as friends and kin
Thought neighbour's service better to begin.
So out we went:—Jane's place was reckon'd good,
Though she 'bout life but little understood,
And had a master wild as wild can be,
And far unfit for such a child as she;
And soon the whisper went about the town,
That Jane's good looks procur'd her many a gown
From him, whose promise was to every one,
But whose intention was to wive with none.
'Twas nought to wonder, though begun by guess;
For Jane was lovely in her Sunday dress,
And all expected such a rosy face
Would be her ruin—as was just the case.
The while the change was easily perceiv'd,
Some months went by, ere I the tales believ'd;
For there are people nowadays, Lord knows,
Will sooner hatch up lies than mend their clothes:
And when with such-like tattle they begin,
Don't mind whose character they spoil a pin:
But passing neighbours often mark'd them smile,
And watch'd him take her milkpail o'er a stile;
And many a time, as wandering closer by,
From Jenny's bosom met a heavy sigh;
And often mark'd her, as discoursing deep,
When doubts might rise to give just cause to weep,
Smothering their notice, by a wish'd disguise
To slive her apron corner to her eyes.
Such signs were mournful and alarming things,
And far more weighty than conjecture brings;

Though foes made double what they heard of all,
Swore lies as proofs, and prophesied her fall.
Poor thoughtless wench! it seems but Sunday past
Since we went out together for the last,
And plain enough indeed it was to find
She'd something more than common on her mind;
For she was always fond and full of chat,
In passing harmless jokes 'bout beaus and that,
But nothing then was scarcely talk'd about,
And what there was, I even forc'd it out.
A gloomy wanness spoil'd her rosy cheek,
And doubts hung there it was not mine to seek;
She ne'er so much as mention'd things to come,
But sigh'd o'er pleasures ere she left her home;
And now and then a mournful smile would raise
At freaks repeated of our younger days,
Which I brought up, while passing spots of ground
Where we, when children, "hurly-burly'd" round,
Or "blindman-buff'd" some morts of hours away—
Two games, poor thing, Jane dearly lov'd to play.
She smil'd at these, but shook her head and sigh'd
Whene'er she thought my look was turn'd aside;
Nor turn'd she round, as was her former way,
To praise the thorn, white over then with May;
Nor stooped once, tho' thousands round her grew,
To pull a cowslip as she us'd to do:
For Jane in flowers delighted from a child—
I like the garden, but she lov'd the wild—
And oft on Sundays young men's gifts declin'd,
Posies from gardens of the sweetest kind,
And eager scrambled the dog-rose to get,
And woodbine-flowers at every bush she met.
The cowslip blossom, with its ruddy streak,
Would tempt her furlongs from the path to seek;
And gay long purple, with its tufty spike,
She'd wade o'er shoes to reach it in the dyke;

And oft, while scratching through the briary woods
For tempting cuckoo-flowers and violet buds,
Poor Jane, I've known her crying sneak to town,
Fearing her mother when she'd torn her gown.
Ah, these were days her conscience view'd with pain,
Which all are loth to lose, as well as Jane.
And, what I took more odd than all the rest,
Was, that same night she ne'er a wish exprest
To see the gipsies, so belov'd before,
That lay a stone's throw from us on the moor:
I hinted it; she just reply'd again—
She once believ'd them, but had doubts since then.
And when we sought our cows, I call'd, "Come
        mull!"
But she stood silent, for her heart was full.
She lov'd dumb things; and ere she had begun
To milk, caress'd them more than e'er she'd done;
But though her tears stood watering in her eye,
I little took it as her last good-bye;
For she was tender, and I've often known
Her mourn when beetles have been trampled on:
So I ne'er dream'd from this, what soon befell,
Till the next morning rang her passing-bell.
My story's long, but time's in plenty yet,
Since the black clouds betoken nought but wet;
And I'll e'en snatch a minute's breath or two,
And take another pinch, to help me through.

'So, as I said, next morn I heard the bell,
And passing neighbours cross'd the street, to tell
That my poor partner Jenny had been found
In the old flag-pool, on the pasture, drown'd.
God knows my heart! I twitter'd like a leaf,
And found too late the cause of Sunday's grief;
For every tongue was loos'd to gabble o'er
The slanderous things that secret pass'd before:

With truth or lies they need not then be strict,
The one they rail'd at could not contradict.
'Twas now no secret of her being beguil'd,
For every mouth knew Jenny died with child ;
And though more cautious with a living name,
Each more than guess'd her master bore the blame.
That very morning, it affects me still,
Ye know the foot-path sidles down the hill,
Ign'rant as babe unborn I pass'd the pond
To milk as usual in our close beyond,
And cows were drinking at the water's edge,
And horses brows'd among the flags and sedge,
And gnats and midges danc'd the water o'er,
Just as I've mark'd them scores of times before,
And birds sat singing as in mornings gone,—
While I as unconcern'd went soodling on,
But little dreaming, as the wakening wind
Flapp'd the broad ash-leaves o'er the pond reclin'd,
And o'er the water crink'd the curdled wave,
That Jane was sleeping in her watery grave.
The neatherd boy that us'd to tend the cows,
While getting whip-sticks from the dangling boughs
Of osiers drooping by the water-side,
Her bonnet floating on the top espied ;
He knew it well, and hasten'd fearful down
To take the terror of his fears to town,—
A melancholy story, far too true ;
And soon the village to the pasture flew,
Where, from the deepest hole the pond about,
They dragg'd poor Jenny's lifeless body out,
And took her home, where scarce an hour gone by
She had been living like to you and I.
I went with more, and kiss'd her for the last,
And thought with tears on pleasures that were past ;
And, the last kindness left me then to do,
I went, at milking, where the blossoms grew,

And handfuls got of rose and lambtoe sweet,
And put them with her in her winding-sheet.
A wilful murder, jury made the crime;
Nor parson 'low'd to pray, nor bell to chime;
On the cross roads, far from her friends and kin,
The usual law for their ungodly sin
Who violent hands upon themselves have laid,
Poor Jane's last bed unchristian-like was made;
And there, like all whose last thoughts turn to
       heaven,
She sleeps, and doubtless hop'd to be forgiven.
But, though I say 't, for maids thus 'veigl'd in
I think the wicked men deserve the sin;
And sure enough we all at last shall see
The treachery punish'd as it ought to be.
For ere his wickedness pretended love,
Jane, I'll be bound, was spotless as the dove,
And 's good a servant, still old folks allow,
As ever scour'd a pail or milk'd a cow;
And ere he led her into ruin's way,
As gay and buxom as a summer's day:
The birds that ranted in the hedge-row boughs,
As night and morning we have sought our cows,
With yokes and buckets as she bounc'd along,
Were often deaf'd to silence with her song.
But now she's gone:—girls, shun deceitful men,
The worst of stumbles ye can fall again';
Be deaf to them, and then, as 'twere, ye'll see
Your pleasures safe as under lock and key.
Throw not my words away, as many do;
They're gold in value, though they're cheap to you.
And husseys hearken, and be warn'd from this,
If ye love mothers, never do amiss:
Jane might love hers, but she forsook the plan
To make her happy, when she thought of man.
Poor tottering dame, it was too plainly known

Her daughter's dying hasten'd on her own,
For from the day the tidings reach'd her door
She took to bed and looked up no more,
And, ere again another year came round,
She, well as Jane, was laid within the ground ;
And all were griev'd poor Goody's end to see :
No better neighbour enter'd house than she,
A harmless soul, with no abusive tongue,
Trig as new pins, and tight 's the day was long ;
And go the week about, nine times in ten
Ye'd find her house as cleanly as her sen.
But, Lord protect us ! time such change does bring,
We cannot dream what o'er our heads may hing ;
The very house she liv'd in, stick and stone,
Since Goody died, has tumbled down and gone :
And where the marjoram once, and sage, and rue,
And balm, and mint, with curl'd-leaf parsley grew,
And double marygolds, and silver thyme,
And pumpkins 'neath the window us'd to climb ;
And where I often when a child for hours
Tried through the pales to get the tempting flowers,
As lady's laces, everlasting peas,
True-love-lies-bleeding, with the hearts-at-ease,
And golden rods, and tansy running high
That o'er the pale-tops smil'd on passers-by,
Flowers in my time that every one would praise,
Tho' thrown like weeds from gardens nowadays ;
Where these all grew, now henbane stinks and
        spreads,
And docks and thistles shake their seedy heads,
And yearly keep with nettles smothering o'er ;—
The house, the dame, the garden known no more :
While, neighbouring nigh, one lonely elder-tree
Is all that 's left of what had us'd to be,
Marking the place, and bringing up with tears
The recollections of one's younger years.

And now I've done, ye're each at once as free
To take your trundle as ye us'd to be;
To take right ways, as Jenny should have ta'en,
Or headlong run, and be a second Jane;
For by one thoughtless girl that's acted ill
A thousand may be guided if they will:
As oft 'mong folks to labour bustling on,
We mark the foremost kick against a stone,
Or stumble o'er a stile he meant to climb,
While hind ones see and shun the fall in time.
But ye, I will be bound, like far the best
Love's tickling nick-nacks and the laughing jest,
And ten times sooner than be warn'd by me,
Would each be sitting on some fellow's knee,
Sooner believe the lies wild chaps will tell
Than old dames' cautions who would wish ye well:
So have your wills.'—She pinch'd her box again,
And ceas'd her tale, and listen'd to the rain,
Which still as usual patter'd fast around,
And bow'd the bent-head loaded to the ground;
While larks, their naked nest by force forsook,
Prun'd their wet wings in bushes by the brook.
The maids, impatient now old Goody ceas'd,
As restless children from the school releas'd,
Right gladly proving, what she'd just foretold,
That young one's stories were preferr'd to old,
Turn to the whisperings of their former joy,
That oft deceive, but very rarely cloy.

RECOLLECTIONS AFTER AN EVENING WALK

JUST as the even-bell rang, we set out
To wander the fields and the meadows about;
And the first thing we mark'd that was lovely to view,
Was the sun hung on nothing, just bidding adieu:
He seem'd like a ball of pure gold in the west,
In a cloud like a mountain blue, dropping to rest;
The skies all around him were ting'd with his rays,
And the trees at a distance seem'd all on a blaze,
Till, lower and lower, he sank from our sight,
And the blue mist came creeping with silence and
        night.
The woodman then ceas'd with his hatchet to hack,
And bent away home with his kid on his back;
The mower too lapt up his scythe from our sight,
And put on his jacket, and bid us good-night;
The thresher once lumping, we heard him no more,
He left his barn-dust, and had shut up his door;
The shepherd had told all his sheep in his pen,
And humming his song, sought his cottage agen:
But the sweetest of all seeming music to me,
Were the songs of the clumsy brown-beetle and bee;
The one was seen hast'ning away to his hive,
The other was just from his sleeping alive,—
'Gainst our hats he kept knocking as if he'd no eyes,
And when batter'd down he was puzzled to rise.
The little gay moth too was lovely to view,
A-dancing with lily-white wings in the dew;
He whisk'd o'er the water-pudge flirting and airy,
And perch'd on the down-headed grass like a fairy.
And there came the snail from his shell peeping out,
As fearful and cautious as thieves on the rout;

The sly jumping frog too had ventur'd to tramp,
And the glow-worm had just 'gun to light up his
    lamp;
To sip of the dew the worm peep'd from his den,
But dreading our footsteps soon vanish'd agen:
And numbers of creatures appear'd in our sight,
That live in the silence and sweetness of night,
Climbing up the tall grasses or scaling the bough,
But these were all nameless, unnotic'd till now.
And then we wound round 'neath the brook's willow
    row,
And look'd at the clouds that kept passing below;
The moon's image too, in the brook we could see 't,
As if 'twas the other world under our feet;
And we listen'd well pleas'd at the guggles and groans
The water made passing the pebbles and stones.
And then we turn'd up by the rut-rifted lane,
And sought for our cot and the village again;
For night gather'd round, and shut all from the eye,
And a black sultry cloud crept all over the sky;
The dew on the bush, soon as touch'd it would drop,
And the grass 'neath our feet was as wet as a mop:
And, as to the town we approach'd very fast,
The bat even popp'd in our face as he past;
And the crickets sang loud as we went by the house,
And by the barn-side we saw many a mouse
Quirking round for the kernels that, litter'd about,
Were shook from the straw which the thresher
    hurl'd out.
And then we came up to our cottage once more,
And shut out the night-dew, and lock'd up the door;
The dog bark'd a welcome, well-pleas'd at our sight,
And the owl o'er our cot flew, and whoop'd a
    'good-night.'

COWPER GREEN

Now eve's hours hot noon succeed;
And day's herald, wing'd with speed,
Flush'd with summer's ruddy face,
Hies to light some cooler place.
Now industry her hand has dropt:
And the din of labour's stopt;
All is silent, free from care,
The welcome boon of night to share.

Pleas'd I wander from the town,
Pester'd by the selfish clown,
Whose talk, though spun the night about,
Hogs, cows, and horses spin it out.
Far from these, so low, so vain,
Glad I wind me down the lane,
Where a deeper gloom pervades
'Tween the hedges' narrow shades;
Where a mimic night-hour spreads,
'Neath the ash-grove's meeting heads.
Onward then I glad proceed,
Where the insect and the weed
Court my eye, as I pursue
Something curious, worthy view:
Chiefly, though, my wanderings bend
Where the groves of ashes end,
And their ceasing lights the scene
Of thy lov'd prospects, Cowper Green!

Though no rills with sandy sweep
Down thy shaggy borders creep,
Save as when thy rut-gull'd lanes
Run little brooks with hasty rains;
Though no yellow plains allow
Food on thee for sheep or cow;

Where on list'ning ears so sweet
Fall the mellow low and bleat,
Greeting, on eve's dewy gale,
Resting-fold and milking-pail;
Though not these adorn thy scene,
Still I love thee, Cowper Green!
Some may praise the grass-plat whims,
Which the gard'ner weekly trims;
And cut-hedge and lawn adore,
Which his shears have smoothen'd o'er:
But give me to ponder still
Nature, when she blooms at will,
In her kindred taste and joy,
Wildness and variety;
Where the furze has leave to wreathe
Its dark prickles o'er the heath;
Where the grey-grown hawthorns spread
Foliag'd houses o'er one's head;
By the spoiling axe untouch'd,
Where the oak tree, gnarl'd and notch'd,
Lifts its deep-moss'd furrow'd side,
In nature's grandeur, nature's pride.
Such is still my favour'd scene,
When I seek thee, Cowper Green!
And full pleas'd would nature's child
Wander o'er thy narrow wild;
Marking well thy shaggy head,
Where uncheck'd the brambles spread;
Where the thistle meets the sight,
With its down-head, cotton-white;
And the nettle, keen to view,
And hemlock with its gloomy hue;
Where the henbane too finds room
For its sickly-stinking bloom;
And full many a nameless weed,
Neglected, left to run to seed,

Seen but with disgust by those
Who judge a blossom by the nose.
Wildness is my suiting scene,
So I seek thee, Cowper Green!

Still thou ought'st to have thy meed,
To show thy flower as well as weed.
Though no fays, from May-day's lap,
Cowslips on thee care to drop;
Still does nature yearly bring
Fairest heralds of the spring:
On thy wood's warm sunny side
Primrose blooms in all its pride;
Violets carpet all thy bowers;
And anemone's weeping flowers,
Dyed in winter's snow and rime,
Constant to their early time,
White the leaf-strewn ground again,
And make each wood a garden then.
Thine's full many a pleasing bloom
Of blossoms lost to all perfume:
Thine the dandelion flowers,
Gilt with dew, like suns with showers;
Hare-bells thine, and bugles blue,
And cuckoo-flowers all sweet to view;
Thy wild-woad on each road we see;
And medicinal betony,
By the woodside-railing, reeves
With antique mullein's flannel-leaves.
These, though mean, the flowers of waste,
Planted here in nature's haste,
Display to the discerning eye
Her loved, wild variety:
Each has charms in nature's book
I cannot pass without a look.
And thou hast fragrant herbs and seed,

Which only garden's culture need:
Thy horehound tufts I love them well,
And ploughman's spikenard's spicy smell;
Thy thyme, strong-scented 'neath one's feet,
Thy marjoram-beds, so doubly sweet;
And pennyroyals creeping twine:
These, each succeeding each, are thine,
Spreading o'er thee wild and gay,
Blessing spring, or summer's day.
As herb, flower, weed adorn thy scene,
Pleas'd I seek thee, Cowper Green.

And I oft zigzag me round
Thy uneven, heathy ground;
Here a knoll and there a scoop
Jostling down and clambering up,
Which the sandman's delving spade
And the pitman's pick have made;
Though many a year has o'er thee roll'd,
Since the grass first hid the mold;
And many a hole has delv'd thee still,
Since peace cloth'd each mimic hill:
Where the pitmen often find
Antique coins of various kind;
And, 'neath many a loosen'd block,
Unlid coffins in the rock,
Casting up the skull and bone
Heedless, as one hurls a stone,
Not a thought of battles by,
Bloody times of chivalry,
When each country's kingly lord
'Gainst his neighbour drew his sword;
And on many a hidden scene,
Now a hamlet, field, or green,
Waged his little bloody fight
To keep his freedom and his right:

And doubtless such was once the scene
Of thee, time-shrouded Cowper Green!
O how I love a glimpse to see
Of hoary, bald antiquity;
And often in my musings sigh,
Whene'er such relics meet my eye,
To think that history's early page
Should yield to black oblivion's rage;
And e'en without a mention made,
Resign them to his deadly shade;
Leaving conjecture but to pause,
That such and such might be the cause.

'Tis sweet the fragments to explore,
Time's so kind to keep in store;
Wrecks the cow-boy often meets
On the mole-hills' thymy seats,
When, by careless pulling weeds,
Chance unbares the shining beads,
That to tasteful minds display
Relics of the Druid day;
Opening on conjecturing eyes
Some lone hermit's paradise.
Doubtless oft, as here it might,
Where such relics meet the sight,
On that self-same spot of ground
Where the cowboy's beads are found,
Hermits, fled from worldly care,
May have moss'd a cottage there;
Liv'd on herbs that there abound,
Food and physic doubly found;
Herbs, that have existence still
In every vale, on every hill,—
Whose virtues only in them died,
As rural life gave way to pride.
Doubtless too oblivion's blot

Blacks some sacred lonely spot,
As 'Cowper Green!' in thee it may,
That once was thine in later day:
Thou mightst hide thy pilgrim then
From the plague of worldly men;
Thou mightst here possess thy cells,
Wholesome herbs, and pilgrim-wells;
And doubtlessly this very seat,
This thyme-capt hill beneath one's feet,
Might be, or nearly so, the spot
On which arose his lonely cot;
And on that existing bank,
Clothed in its sedges rank,
Grass might grow, and mosses spread,
That thatch'd his roof, and made his bed:
Yes, such might be; and such I love
To think and fancy, as I rove
O'er thy wood-encircled hill,
Like a world-shunning pilgrim still.

Now the dew-mists faster fall,
And the night her gloomy pall
Black'ning flings 'tween earth and sky,
Hiding all things from the eye;
Nor broken seam, nor thin spun screen,
The moon can find to peep between:
Now thy unmolested grass,
Untouch'd even by the ass,
Spindled up its destin'd height,
Far too sour for sheep to bite,
Drooping hangs each feeble joint
With a glass nob on its point:—
Fancy now shall leave the scene,
And bid good-night to Cowper Green.

THE WOOD-CUTTER'S NIGHT SONG

WELCOME, red and roundy sun,
  Dropping lowly in the west;
Now my hard day's work is done,
  I'm as happy as the best.

Joyful are the thoughts of home,
  Now I'm ready for my chair,
So, till morrow-morning's come,
  Bill and mittens, lie ye there!

Though to leave your pretty song,
  Little birds, it gives me pain,
Yet to-morrow is not long,
  Then I'm with you all again.

If I stop, and stand about,
  Well I know how things will be,
Judy will be looking out
  Every now-and-then for me.

So fare ye well! and hold your tongues,
  Sing no more until I come;
They're not worthy of your songs
  That never care to drop a crumb.

All day long I love the oaks,
  But, at nights, yon little cot,
Where I see the chimney smokes,
  Is by far the prettiest spot.

Wife and children all are there,
  To revive with pleasant looks,
Table ready set, and chair,
  Supper hanging on the hooks.

Soon as ever I get in,
  When my faggot down I fling,
Little prattlers they begin
  Teasing me to talk and sing.

Welcome, red and roundy sun,
  Dropping lowly in the west;
Now my hard day's work is done,
  I'm as happy as the best.

Joyful are the thoughts of home,
  Now I'm ready for my chair,
So, till morrow-morning's come,
  Bill and mittens, lie ye there!

A PASTORAL

SURELY Lucy love returns,
  Though her meaning's not reveal'd;
Surely love her bosom burns,
  Which her coyness keeps conceal'd:
Else what means that flushing cheek,
  When with her I chance to be?
And those looks, that almost speak
  A secret warmth of love for me?

Would she, where she valued not,
  Give such proofs of sweet esteem?
Think what flowers for me she's got—
  What can this but fondness seem?
When, to try their pleasing powers,
  Swains for her cull every grove,—
When she takes my meaner flowers,
  What can guide the choice but love?

Was not love seen yesternight,
    When two sheep had rambled out?
Who but Lucy set them right?
    The token told, without a doubt.
When others stare, she turns and frowns;
    When I but glance, a smile I see;
When others talk, she calls them clowns;
    But never says such words to me.

And when, with swains to love inclin'd,
    To bear her milk I often go;
Though they beg first, she turns behind,
    And lingers till I ask her too:
O'er stepping-stones that cross the brooks,
    Who mind such trifles plainly see,
In vain the shepherds prop their hooks,
    She always gives her hand to me.

To-day, while all were standing by,
    She wish'd for roses from the bower;
The man too wish'd was in her eye,
    Though others flew to get the flower:
And striving all they could to please,
    When prick'd with thorns they left the tree,
She never seem'd concern'd at these,
    But only turn'd to caution me.

To-day she careless view'd the bark
    Where many a swain had cut her name,
'Till whisper'd which was Colin's mark,
    Her cheek was instant in a flame:
In blushing beckons love did call,
    And courage seiz'd the chance the while;
And though I kiss'd her 'fore them all,
    Her worst rebukings wore a smile.

THE REQUEST

Now the sun his blinking beam
  Behind yon mountain loses,
And each eye, that might evil deem,
  In blinded slumber closes:
Now the field's a desert grown,
  Now the hedger's fled the grove;
Put thou on thy russet gown,
   Shielded from the dews, my love,
     And wander out with me.

We have met at early day,
  Slander rises early,
Slander's tongues had much to say,
  And still I love thee dearly:
Slander now to rest has gone,
  Only wakes the courting dove;
Slily steal thy bonnet on,
   Leave thy father's cot, my love,
     And wander out with me.

Clowns have pass'd our noon-day screen,
  'Neath the hawthorn's blossom,
Seldom there the chance has been
  To press thee to my bosom:
Ploughmen now no more appear,
  Night-winds but the thorn-bough move;
Squander not a minute here,
   Lift the door-latch gently, love,
     And wander out with me.

CLARE   E

Oh the hour so sweet as this,
  With friendly night surrounded,
Left free to talk, embrace, and kiss,
  By virtue only bounded —
Lose it not, make no delay,
  Put on thy doublet, hat, and glove,
Sly ope the door and steal away;
  And sweet 'twill be, my only love,
    To wander out with thee.

SONG

THERE's the daisy, the woodbine,
  And crow-flower so golden;
There's the wild rose, the eglantine,
  And May-buds unfolding;
There are flowers for my fairy,
  And bowers for my love:
Wilt thou gang with me, Mary,
  To the banks of Brooms-grove?

There's the thorn-bush and the ash-tree
  To shield thee from the heat,
While the brook to refresh thee
  Runs close by thy feet;
The thrushes are chanting clear,
  In the pleasures of love;
Thou'rt the only thing wanting here
  'Mid the sweets of Brooms-grove.

Then come ere a minute's gone,
  Since the long summer's day
Puts her wings swift as linnets' on
  For hieing away.

Then come with no doubtings near,
    To fear a false love;
For there's nothing without thee, dear,
    Can please in Brooms-grove.

The woodbine may nauntle here,
    In blossoms so fine,
The wild roses mantling near
    In blushes may shine;
Mary queen of each blossom proves,
    She's the blossom I love,
She's the all that my bosom loves
    'Mong the sweets of Brooms-grove.

SONG

ONE gloomy eve I roam'd about
    'Neath Oxey's hazel bowers,
While timid hares were darting out,
    To crop the dewy flowers;
And soothing was the scene to me,
    Right pleased was my soul,
My breast was calm as summer's sea
    When waves forget to roll.

But short was even's placid smile,
    My startled soul to charm,
When Nelly lightly skipt the stile,
    With milk-pail on her arm:
One careless look on me she flung,
    As bright as parting day;
And like a hawk from covert sprung,
    It pounc'd my peace away.

E 2

SONG

Swamps of wild rush-beds, and sloughs' squashy traces,
 Grounds of rough fallows with thistle and weed,
Flats and low vallies of kingcups and daisies,
 Sweetest of subjects are ye for my reed:
Ye commons left free in the rude rags of nature,
 Ye brown heaths be-clothed in furze as ye be,
My wild eye in rapture adores every feature,
 Ye are dear as this heart in my bosom to me.

O native endearments! I would not forsake ye,
 I would not forsake ye for sweetest of scenes;
For sweetest of gardens that nature could make me,
 I would not forsake ye, dear vallies and greens:
Tho' nature ne'er dropt ye a cloud-resting mountain,
 Nor waterfalls tumble their music so free;
Had nature deny'd ye a bush, tree, or fountain,
 Ye still had been lov'd as an Eden by me.

And long, my dear vallies, long, long may ye flourish,
 Though rush-beds and thistles make most of your
  pride;
May showers never fail the green's daisies to nourish,
 Nor suns dry the fountain that rills by its side.
Your skies may be gloomy, and misty your mornings,
 Your flat swampy vallies unwholesome may be;
Still, refuse of nature, without her adornings
 Ye are dear as this heart in my bosom to me.

IMPROMPTU

'WHERE art thou wandering, little child?'
  I said to one I met to-day—
She push'd her bonnet up and smil'd,
  'I'm going upon the green to play:
Folks tell me that the May's in flower,
  That cowslip-peeps are fit to pull,
And I've got leave to spend an hour
  To get this little basket full.'

—And thou'st got leave to spend an hour!
  My heart repeated—she was gone;
—And thou hast heard the thorn's in flower,
  And childhood's bliss is urging on:
Ah, happy child! thou mak'st me sigh,
  This once as happy heart of mine,
Would nature with the boon comply,
  How gladly would I change for thine.

TO THE BUTTERFLY

LOVELY insect, haste away,
Greet once more the sunny day;
Leave, O leave the murky barn,
Ere trapping spiders thee discern;
Soon as seen, they will beset
Thy golden wings with filmy net,
Then all in vain to set thee free,
Hopes all lost for liberty.
Never think that I belie,
Never fear a winter sky;
Budding oaks may now be seen,
Starry daisies deck the green,
Primrose groups the woods adorn,
Cloudless skies, and blossom'd thorn;

These all prove that spring is here,
Haste away then, never fear.
Skim o'er hill and valley free,
Perch upon the blossom'd tree;
Though my garden would be best,
Couldst thou but contented rest:
There the school-boy has no power
Thee to chase from flower to flower,
Harbour none for cruel sport,
Far away thy foes resort;
Nought is there but liberty,
Pleasant place for thee and me.
Then hither bend thy roving flight,
In my garden take delight.
Though the dew-bent level dale
Rears the lily of the vale,
Though the thicket's bushy dell
Tempts thee to the foxglove's bell,
Come but once within my bounds,
View my garden's airy rounds,
Soon thou'lt find the scene complete,
And every flowret twice as sweet:
Then, lovely insect, come away,
Greet once more the sunny day.
Oft I've seen, when warm and dry,
'Mong the bean-fields bosom-high,
How thy starry gems and gold
To admiration would unfold:
Lo! the arching heavenly bow
Doth all his dyes on thee bestow,
Crimson, blue, and watery green,
Mix'd with azure shade between;
These are thine—thou first in place,
Queen of all the insect race!
And I've often thought, alone,
This to thee was not unknown;

For amid the sunny hour,
When I've found thee on a flower,
(Searching with minutest gleg,)
Oft I've seen thy little leg
Soft as glass o'er velvet glides
Smoothen down thy silken sides;
Then thy wings would ope and shut;
Then thou seemingly wouldst strut:
Was it nature, was it pride?
Let the learned world decide.
Enough for me, (though some may deem
This a trifling, silly theme,)
Wouldst thou in my garden come,
To join the bee's delightful hum;
These silly themes then, day and night,
Should be thy trifler's whole delight.
Then, lovely insect, haste away,
Greet once more the sunny day.

TO THE RURAL MUSE

Simple enchantress! wreath'd in summer blooms
  Of slender bent-stalks topt with feathery down,
Heath's creeping vetch, and glaring yellow brooms,
  With ash-keys wavering on thy rushy crown;
Simple enchantress! how I've woo'd thy smiles,
  How often sought thee far from flush'd renown;
Sought thee unseen where fountain-waters fell;
  Touch'd thy wild reed unheard, in weary toils;
And though my heavy hand thy song defiles,
  'Tis hard to leave thee, and to bid farewell.

Simple enchantress! ah, from all renown,
  Far off, my soul hath warm'd in bliss to see
The varied figures on thy summer-gown,
  That nature's finger works so 'witchingly;

The colour'd flower, the silken leaves that crown
  Green nestling bower-bush, and high towering
    tree;
Brooks of the sunny green and shady dell:
  Ah, sweet full many a time they've been to me;
And though my weak song falters, sung to thee,
  I cannot, wild enchantress, bid farewell.

Still must I seek thee, though I wind the brook
  When morning sunbeams o'er the waters glide,
And trace thy footsteps in the lonely nook
  As evening moists the daisy by thy side;
Ah, though I woo thee on thy bed of thyme,—
  If courting thee be deem'd ambition's pride,
It is so passing sweet with thee to dwell—
  If love for thee in clowns be call'd a crime,
Forgive presumption, O thou queen of rhyme!
  I've lov'd thee long, I cannot bid farewell.

TO AUTUMN

COME, pensive Autumn, with thy clouds, and storms,
  And falling leaves, and pastures lost to flowers;
A luscious charm hangs on thy faded forms,
  More sweet than Summer in her loveliest hours,
Who, in her blooming uniform of green,
  Delights with samely and continued joy:
But give me, Autumn, where thy hand hath been,
  For there is wildness that can never cloy,—
The russet hue of fields left bare, and all
The tints of leaves and blossoms ere they fall.
  In thy dull days of clouds a pleasure comes,
Wild music softens in thy hollow winds;
  And in thy fading woods a beauty blooms,
That's more than dear to melancholy minds.

IN HILLY-WOOD

How sweet to be thus nestling deep in boughs,
   Upon an ashen stoven pillowing me;
Faintly are heard the ploughmen at their ploughs,
   But not an eye can find its way to see.
The sunbeams scarce molest me with a smile,
   So thick the leafy armies gather round;
And where they do, the breeze blows cool the while,
   Their leafy shadows dancing on the ground.
Full many a flower, too, wishing to be seen,
Perks up its head the hiding grass between.—
   In mid-wood silence, thus, how sweet to be;
Where all the noises, that on peace intrude,
   Come from the chittering cricket, bird, and bee,
Whose songs have charms to sweeten solitude.

MORNING

O now the crimson east, its fire-streak burning,
   Tempts me to wander 'neath the blushing morn,
Winding the zig-zag lane, turning and turning,
   As winds the crooked fence's wilder'd thorn.
Where is the eye can gaze upon the blushes,
Unmov'd, with which yon cloudless heaven flushes?
   I cannot pass the very bramble, weeping
'Neath dewy tear-drops that its spears surround,
   Like harlot's mockery on the wan cheek creeping,
Gilding the poison that is meant to wound;—
   I cannot pass the bent, ere gales have shaken
Its transient crowning off, each point adorning,—
   But all the feelings of my soul awaken,
To own the witcheries of most lovely Morning.

TO AN HOUR-GLASS

OLD-FASHIONED uncouth measurer of the day,
  I love to watch thy filtering burthen pass;
Though some there are that live would bid thee stay;
  But these view reasons through a different glass
From him, Time's meter, who addresses thee.
  The world has joys which they may deem as such;
The world has wealth to season vanity,
  And wealth is theirs to make their vainness much:
But small to do with joys and Fortune's fee
Hath he, Time's chronicler, who welcomes thee.
  So jog thou on, through hours of doom'd distress;
So haste thou on the glimpse of hopes to come;
  As every sand-grain counts a trouble less,
As every drain'd glass leaves me nearer home.

AFTER READING IN A LETTER

PROPOSALS FOR BUILDING A COTTAGE

BESIDE a runnel build my shed,
  With stubbles cover'd o'er;
Let broad oaks o'er its chimney spread,
  And grass-plats grace the door.

The door may open with a string,
  So that it closes tight;
And locks would be a wanted thing,
  To keep out thieves at night.

A little garden, not too fine,
  Inclose with painted pales;
And woodbines, round the cot to twine,
  Pin to the wall with nails.

Let hazels grow, and spindling sedge,
  Bend bowering over-head;
Dig old man's beard from woodland hedge,
  To twine a summer shade.

Beside the threshold sods provide,
  And build a summer seat;
Plant sweet-briar bushes by its side,
  And flowers that blossom sweet.

I love the sparrow's ways to watch
  Upon the cotter's sheds,
So here and there pull out the thatch,
  That they may hide their heads.

And as the sweeping swallows stop
  Their flights along the green,
Leave holes within the chimney-top
  To paste their nest between.

Stick shelves and cupboards round the hut,
  In all the holes and nooks;
Nor in the corner fail to put
  A cupboard for the books.

Along the floor some sand I'll sift,
  To make it fit to live in;
And then I'll thank ye for the gift,
  As something worth the giving.

SOLITUDE

Now as even's warning bell
Rings the day's departing knell,
Leaving me from labour free,
Solitude, I'll walk with thee:
Whether 'side the woods we rove,
Or sweep beneath the willow grove;
Whether sauntering we proceed

Cross the green, or down the mead;
Whether, sitting down, we look
On the bubbles of the brook;
Whether, curious, waste an hour,
Pausing o'er each tasty flower;
Or, expounding nature's spells,
From the sand pick out the shells;
Or, while lingering by the streams,
Where more sweet the music seems,
Listen to the soft'ning swells
Of some distant chiming bells
Mellowing sweetly on the breeze,
Rising, falling by degrees,
Dying now, then wak'd again
In full many a 'witching strain,
Sounding, as the gale flits by,
Flats and sharps of melody.

Sweet it is to wind the rill,
Sweet with thee to climb the hill,
On whose lap the bullock free
Chews his cud most placidly;
Or o'er fallows bare and brown
Beaten sheep-tracks wander down,
Where the mole unwearied still
Roots up many a crumbling hill,
And the little chumbling mouse
Gnarls the dead weed for her house,
While the plough's unfeeling share
Lays full many a dwelling bare;—
Where the lark with russet breast
'Hind the big clod hides her nest,
And the black snail's founder'd pace
Finds from noon a hiding-place,
Breaking off the scorching sun
Where the matted twitches run.

Solitude! I love thee well,
Brushing through the wilder'd dell,
Picking from the ramping grass
Nameless blossoms as I pass,
Which the dews of eve bedeck,
Fair as pearls on woman's neck;
Marking shepherds rous'd from sleep
Blundering off to fold their sheep;
And the swain, with toils distrest,
Hide his tools to seek his rest:
While the cows, with hobbling strides,
Twitching slow their fly-bit hides,
Rub the pasture's creaking gate,
Milking maids and boys to wait.
Or as sunshine leaves the sky,
As the daylight shuts her eye,
Sweet it is to meet the breeze
'Neath the shade of hawthorn trees,
By the pasture's wilder'd round,
Where the pismire hills abound,
Where the blushing fin-weed's flower
Closes up at even's hour:
Leaving then the green behind,
Narrow hoof-plod lanes to wind,
Oak and ash embower'd beneath,
Leading to the lonely heath,
Where the unmolested furze
And the burdock's clinging burs,
And the briars, by freedom sown,
Claim the wilder'd spots their own

There while we the scene survey
Deck'd in nature's wild array,
Swell'd with ling-clad hillocks green
Suiting the disorder'd scene,
Haply we may rest us then

In the banish'd herdsman's den;
Where the wattled hulk is fixt,
Propt some double oak betwixt,
Where the swain the branches lops,
And o'er head with rushes tops;
Where, with woodbine's sweet perfume,
And the rose's blushing bloom,
Loveliest cieling of the bower,
Arching in, peeps many a flower;
While a hill of thyme so sweet,
Or a moss'd stone, forms a seat.
There, as 'tween-light hangs the eve,
I will watch thy bosom heave;
Marking then the darksome flows
Night's gloom o'er thy mantle throws;
Fondly gazing on thine eye
As it rolls its extasy,
When thy solemn musings caught
Tell thy soul's absorb'd in thought;
When thy finely folded arm
O'er thy bosom beating warm
Wraps thee melancholy round;
And thy ringlets wild unbound
On thy lily shoulders lie,
Like dark streaks in morning's sky.
Peace and silence sit with thee,
And peace alone is heaven to me:
While the moonlight's infant hour
Faint 'gins creep to gild the bower,
And the wattled hedge gleams round
Its diamond shadows on the ground.
—O thou soothing Solitude,
From the vain and from the rude,
When this silent hour is come,
And I meet thy welcome home,
What balm is thine to troubles deep,

As on thy breast I sink to sleep;
What bliss on even's silence flows,
When thy wish'd opiate brings repose.

And I have found thee wondrous sweet,
Sheltering from the noon-day heat,
As 'neath hazels I have stood
In the gloomy hanging wood,
Where the sunbeams, filtering small,
Freckling through the branches fall;
And the flapping leaf the ground
Shadows, flitting round and round:
Where the glimmering streamlets wreathe
Many a crooked root beneath,
Unseen gliding day by day
O'er their solitary way,
Smooth or rough, as onward led
Where the wild-weed dips its head,
Murmuring,—dribbling drop by drop
When dead leaves their progress stop,—
Or winding sweet their restless way
While the frothy bubbles play.
And I love thy presence drear
In such wildernesses, where
Ne'er an axe was heard to sound,
Or a tree's fall gulsh'd the ground,
Where (as if that spot could be)
First foot-mark'd the ground by me,
All is still, and wild, and gay,
Left as at creation's day.
Pleasant too it is to look
For thy steps in shady nook,
Where, by hedge-side coolly led,
Brooks curl o'er their sandy bed;
On whose tide the clouds reflect,
In whose margin flags are freckt;

Where the waters, winding blue,
Single-arch'd brig flutter through,
While the willow-branches grey
Damp the sultry eye of day,
And in whispers mildly sooth
Chafe the mossy keystone smooth;
Where the banks, beneath them spread,
Level in an easy bed;
While the wild-thyme's pinky bells
Circulate reviving smells;
And the breeze, with feather-feet,
Crimping o'er the waters sweet,
Trembling fans the sun-tann'd cheek,
And gives the comfort one would seek.
Stretching there in soft repose,
Far from peace and freedom's foes,
In a spot, so wild, so rude,
Dear to me is solitude!
Soothing then to watch the ground,—
Every insect flitting round,
Such as painted summer brings;—
Lady-fly with freckled wings,
Watch her up the tall bent climb;
And from knotted flowers of thyme,
Where the woodland banks are deckt,
See the bee his load collect;
Mark him turn the petals by,
Gold dust gathering on his thigh,
As full many a hum he heaves,
While he pats th' intruding leaves,
Lost in many a heedless spring,
Then wearing home on heavy wing.

But when sorrows more oppress.
When the world brings more distress,
Wishing to despise as then

Brunts of fate, and scorn of men;
When fate's demons thus intrude.
Then I seek thee, Solitude,
Where the abbey's height appears
Hoary 'neath a weight of years;
Where the mouldering walls are seen
Hung with pellitory green;
Where the steeple's taper stretch
Tires the eye its length to reach,
Dizzy, nauntling high and proud,
Top-stone losing in a cloud;
Where the cross, to time resign'd,
Creaking harshly in the wind,
Crowning high the rifted dome,
Points the pilgrim's wish'd-for home;
While the look fear turns away,
Shuddering at its dread decay.
There let me my peace pursue
'Neath the shades of gloomy yew,
Doleful hung with mourning green,
Suiting well the solemn scene;
There, that I may learn to scan
Mites illustrious, called man,
Turn with thee the nettles by
Where the grave-stone meets the eye,
Soon, full soon to read and see
That all below is vanity;
And man, to me a galling thing,
Own'd creation's lord and king,
A minute's length, a zephyr's breath,
Sport of fate, and prey of death;
Tyrant to-day, to-morrow gone;
Distinguish'd only by a stone,
That fain would have the eye to know
Pride's better dust is lodg'd below,—
While worms like me are mouldering laid,

With nothing set to say 'they're dead;'—
All the difference, trifling thing,
That notes at last the slave and king.
As wither'd leaves, life's bloom when stopt,
That drop in autumn, so they dropt:
As snails, which in their painted shell
So snugly once were known to dwell,
When in the school-boy's care we view
The pleasing toys of varied hue.—
By age or accident are flown,
The shell left empty,—tenant gone;—
So pass we from the world's affairs,
And careless vanish from its cares;
So leave, with silent, long farewell,
Vain life—as left the snail his shell.

All this when there my eyes behold
On every stone and heap of mould,
Solitude, though thou art sweet,
Solemn art thou then to meet;
When with list'ning pause I look
Round the pillar's ruin'd nook,
Glooms revealing, dim descried,
Ghosts, companion'd by thy side;
Where in old deformity
Ancient arches sweep on high;
And the aisles, to light unknown,
Create a darkness all their own:
Save the moon, as on we pass,
Splinters through the broken glass,
Or the torn roof, patch'd with cloud,
Or the crack'd wall, bulg'd and bow'd,—
Glimmering faint along the ground,
Shooting solemn and profound,
Lighting up the silent gloom
Just to read an ancient tomb:

'Neath where, as it gilding creeps,
We may see some abbot sleeps;
And as on we mete the aisle,
Daring scarce to breathe the while,
Soft as creeping feet can fall,
While the damp green-stained wall
Swift the startled ghost flits by,
Mocking murmurs faintly sigh;
Reminding our intruding fear
Such visits are unwelcome here.
Seemly then, from hollow urn,
Gentle steps our steps return:
E'er so soft and e'er so still,
Check our breath or how we will,
List'ning spirits still reply
Step for step, and sigh for sigh.
Murmuring o'er one's weary woe,
Such as once 'twas theirs to know,
They whisper to such slaves as me,
A buried tale of misery:—
'We once had life, ere life's decline,
Flesh, blood, and bones, the same as thine;
We knew its pains, and shar'd its grief,
Till death, long wish'd-for, brought relief;
We had our hopes, and like to thee,
Hop'd morrow's better day to see,
But like to thine, our hope the same,
To-morrow's kindness never came:
We had our tyrants, e'en as thou;
Our wants met many a scornful brow;
But death laid low their wealthy powers,
Their harmless ashes mix with ours:
And this vain world, its pride, its form,
That treads on thee as on a worm,
Its mighty heirs—the time shall be
When they as quiet sleep by thee!'

O here's thy comfort, Solitude,
When overpowering woes intrude!
Then thy sad, thy solemn dress
Owns the balm my soul to bless:
Here I judge the world aright;
Here see vain man in his true light;
Learn patience, in this trying hour,
To gild life's brambles with a flower;
Take pattern from the hints thou'st given,
And follow in thy steps to heaven.

BALLAD

WINTER's gone, the summer breezes
   Breathe the shepherd's joys again,
Village scene no longer pleases,
   Pleasures meet upon the plain;
Snows are fled that hung the bowers,
   Buds to blossoms softly steal,
Winter's rudeness melts in flowers:—
     Charmer, leave thy spinning wheel,
       And tend the sheep with me.

Careless here shall pleasures lull thee,
   From domestic troubles free;
Rushes for thy couch I'll pull thee,
   In the shade thy seat shall be;
All the flower-buds will I get
   Spring's first sunbeams do unseal,
Primrose, cowslip, violet:—
     Charmer, leave thy spinning wheel,
       And tend the sheep with me.

Cast away thy 'twilly willy,'
   Winter's warm protecting gown,
Storms no longer blow to chill thee;
   Come with mantle loosely thrown,

Garments, light as gale's embraces,
  That thy lovely shape reveal;
Put thou on thy airy dresses:—
    Charmer, leave thy spinning wheel,
        And tend the sheep with me.

Sweet to sit where brooks are flowing,
  Pleasant spreads the gentle heat,
On the green's lap thyme is growing,
  Every molehill forms a seat:
Fear not suns 'cause thou'rt so fair,
  In the thorn-bower we'll conceal;
Ne'er a sunbeam pierces there:—
    Charmer, leave thy spinning wheel,
        And tend the sheep with me.

FEBRUARY

I

THE snow has left the cottage top;
  The thatch-moss grows in brighter green;
And eaves in quick succession drop,
  Where grinning icicles have been,
Pit-patting with a pleasant noise
  In tubs set by the cottage-door;
While ducks and geese, with happy joys,
  Plunge in the yard-pond brimming o'er.

II

The sun peeps through the window-pane,
  Which children mark with laughing eye,
And in the wet street steal again,
  To tell each other Spring is nigh:
Then, as young hope the past recalls,
  In playing groups they often draw,
To build beside the sunny walls
  Their spring-time huts of sticks or straw.

III

And oft in pleasure's dreams they hie
　　Round homesteads by the village side,
Scratching the hedgerow mosses by,
　　Where painted pooty-shells abide;
Mistaking oft the ivy spray
　　For leaves that come with budding Spring,
And wond'ring, in their search for play,
　　Why birds delay to build and sing.

IV

The milkmaid singing leaves her bed,
　　As glad as happy thoughts can be,
While magpies chatter o'er her head
　　As jocund in the change as she:
Her cows around the closes stray,
　　Nor ling'ring wait the foddering-boy;
Tossing the mole-hills in their play,
　　And staring round with frolic joy.

V

The shepherd now is often seen
　　Near warm banks o'er his hook to bend;
Or o'er a gate or stile to lean,
　　Chattering to a passing friend:
Ploughmen go whistling to their toils,
　　And yoke again the rested plough;
And, mingling o'er the mellow soils,
　　Boys shout, and whips are noising now.

VI

The barking dogs, by lane and wood,
　　Drive sheep a-field from foddering ground;
And Echo, in her summer mood,
　　Briskly mocks the cheering sound.

The flocks, as from a prison broke,
  Shake their wet fleeces in the sun,
While, following fast, a misty smoke
  Reeks from the moist grass as they run.

VII

No more behind his master's heels
  The dog creeps on his winter-pace;
But cocks his tail, and o'er the fields
  Runs many a wild and random chase,
Following, in spite of chiding calls,
  The startled cat with harmless glee,
Scaring her up the weed-green walls,
  Or mossy mottled apple tree.

VIII

As crows from morning perches fly,
  He barks and follows them in vain;
E'en larks will catch his nimble eye,
  And off he starts and barks again,
With breathless haste and blinded guess,
  Oft following where the hare hath gone;
Forgetting, in his joy's excess,
  His frolic puppy-days are done!

IX

The hedgehog, from his hollow root,
  Sees the wood-moss clear of snow,
And hunts the hedge for fallen fruit—
  Crab, hip, and winter-bitten sloe;
But often check'd by sudden fears,
  As shepherd-dog his haunt espies,
He rolls up in a ball of spears,
  And all his barking rage defies.

X

The gladden'd swine bolt from the sty,
  And round the yard in freedom run,
Or stretching in their slumbers lie
  Beside the cottage in the sun.
The young horse whinneys to his mate,
  And, sickening from the thresher's door,
Rubs at the straw-yard's banded gate,
  Longing for freedom on the moor.

XI

The small birds think their wants are o'er,
  To see the snow-hills fret again,
And, from the barn's chaff-litter'd door,
  Betake them to the greening plain.
The woodman's robin startles coy,
  Nor longer to his elbow comes,
To peck, with hunger's eager joy,
  'Mong mossy stulps the litter'd crumbs.

XII

'Neath hedge and walls that screen the wind,
  The gnats for play will flock together;
And e'en poor flies some hope will find
  To venture in the mocking weather;
From out their hiding-holes again,
  With feeble pace, they often creep
Along the sun-warm'd window-pane,
  Like dreaming things that walk in sleep.

XIII

The mavis thrush with wild delight,
  Upon the orchard's dripping tree,
Mutters, to see the day so bright,
  Fragments of young Hope's poesy:

And oft Dame stops her buzzing wheel
  To hear the robin's note once more,
Who tootles while he pecks his meal
  From sweet-briar hips beside the door.

XIV

The sunbeams on the hedges lie,
  The south wind murmurs summer soft;
The maids hang out white clothes to dry
  Around the elder-skirted croft:
A calm of pleasure listens round,
  And almost whispers Winter by;
While Fancy dreams of Summer's sound,
  And quiet rapture fills the eye.

XV

Thus Nature of the Spring will dream
  While south winds thaw; but soon again
Frost breathes upon the stiff'ning stream,
  And numbs it into ice: the plain
Soon wears its mourning garb of white;
  And icicles, that fret at noon,
Will eke their icy tails at night
  Beneath the chilly stars and moon.

XVI

Nature soon sickens of her joys,
  And all is sad and dumb again,
Save merry shouts of sliding boys
  About the frozen furrow'd plain.
The foddering-boy forgets his song,
  And silent goes with folded arms;
And croodling shepherds bend along,
  Crouching to the whizzing storms.

APRIL

I

Now infant April joins the Spring,
   And views the watery sky,
As youngling linnet tries its wing,
   And fears at first to fly;
With timid step she ventures on,
   And hardly dares to smile,
Till blossoms open one by one,
   And sunny hours beguile.

II

But finer days are coming yet,
   With scenes more sweet to charm,
And suns arrive that rise and set,
   Bright strangers to a storm:
Then, as the birds with louder song
   Each morning's glory cheer,
With bolder step she speeds along,
   And loses all her fear.

III

In wanton gambols, like a child,
   She tends her early toils,
And seeks the buds along the wild,
   That blossoms while she smiles;
Or, laughing on, with nought to chide,
   She races with the Hours,
Or sports by Nature's lovely side,
   And fills her lap with flowers.

IV

The shepherd on his pasture walks
   The first fair cowslip finds,
Whose tufted flowers, on slender stalks,
   Keep nodding to the winds.

And though the thorns withhold the May,
  Their shades the violets bring,
Which children stoop for in their play
  As tokens of the Spring.

v

Those joys which childhood calls its own,
  Would they were kin to men!
Those treasures to the world unknown,
  When known, are wither'd then!
But hovering round our growing years,
  To gild Care's sable shroud,
Their spirit through the gloom appears
  As suns behind a cloud.

VI

Since thou didst meet my infant eyes,
  As through the fields I flew,
Whose distance, where they meet the skies,
  Was all the world I knew;
That warmth of Fancy's wildest hours,
  Which fill'd all things with life,
Which heard a voice in trees and flowers,
  Has swoon'd in Reason's strife.

VII

Sweet Month! thy pleasures bid thee be
  The fairest child of Spring;
And every hour, that comes with thee,
  Comes some new joy to bring:
The trees still deepen in their bloom,
  Grass greens the meadow-lands,
And flowers with every morning come,
  As dropt by fairy hands.

VIII

The field and garden's lovely hours
    Begin and end with thee;
For what's so sweet, as peeping flowers
    And bursting buds to see,
What time the dew's unsullied drops,
    In burnish'd gold, distil
On crocus flowers' unclosing tops,
    And drooping daffodil?

IX

To see thee come, all hearts rejoice;
    And, warm with feelings strong,
With thee all Nature finds a voice,
    And hums a waking song.
The lover views thy welcome hours,
    And thinks of summer come,
And takes the maid thy early flowers,
    To tempt her steps from home.

X

Along each hedge and sprouting bush
    The singing birds are blest,
And linnet green and speckled thrush
    Prepare their mossy nest;
On the warm bed thy plains supply,
    The young lambs find repose,
And 'mid thy green hills basking lie
    Like spots of ling'ring snows.

XI

Thy open'd leaves and ripen'd buds
    The cuckoo makes his choice,
And shepherds in thy greening woods
    First hear his cheering voice:

And to thy ripen'd blooming bowers
  The nightingale belongs;
And, singing to thy parting hours,
  Keeps night awake with songs!

XII

With thee the swallow dares to come,
  And cool his sultry wing;
And, urged to seek his yearly home,
  Thy suns the martin bring.
Oh! lovely Month! be leisure mine
  Thy yearly mate to be;
Though May-day scenes may brighter shine,
  Their birth belongs to thee.

XIII

I waked me with thy rising sun,
  And thy first glories viewed,
And, as thy welcome hours begun,
  Their sunny steps pursued.
And now thy sun is on thee set,
  Like to a lovely eve,
I view thy parting with regret,
  And linger loth to leave.

XIV

Though at her birth the northern gale
  Come with its withering sigh;
And hopeful blossoms, turning pale,
  Upon her bosom die;
Ere April seeks another place,
  And ends her reign in this,
She leaves us with as fair a face
  As e'er gave birth to bliss!

JULY

July, the month of Summer's prime,
Again resumes his busy time;
Scythes tinkle in each grassy dell,
Where solitude was wont to dwell;
And meadows, they are mad with noise
Of laughing maids and shouting boys,
Making up the withering hay
With merry hearts as light as play.
The very insects on the ground
So nimbly bustle all around,
Among the grass, or dusty soil,
They seem partakers in the toil.
The landscape even reels with life,
While 'mid the busy stir and strife
Of industry, the shepherd still
Enjoys his summer dreams at will,
Bent o'er his hook, or listless laid
Beneath the pasture's willow shade,
Whose foliage shines so cool and gray
Amid the sultry hues of day,
As if the morning's misty veil
Yet linger'd in its shadows pale;
Or lolling in a musing mood
On mounds where Saxon castles stood,
Upon whose deeply-buried walls
The ivy'd oak's dark shadow falls,
He oft picks up with wond'ring gaze
Some little thing of other days,
Saved from the wrecks of time—as beads,
Or broken pots among the weeds,
Of curious shapes—and many a stone
From Roman pavements thickly strown,
Oft hoping, as he searches round,
That buried riches may be found.

Though, search as often as he will,
His hopes are disappointed still;
Or watching, on his mossy seat,
The insect world beneath his feet,
In busy motion here and there
Like visitors to feast or fair,
Some climbing up the rush's stem,
A steeple's height or more to them,
With speed, that sees no fear to stop,
Till perch'd upon its spiry top,
Where they awhile the view survey,
Then prune their wings, and flit away,—
And others journeying to and fro
Among the grassy woods below,
Musing, as if they felt and knew
The pleasant scenes they wander'd through,
Where each bent round them seems to be
Huge as a giant timber-tree.
Shaping the while their dark employs
To his own visionary joys,
He pictures such a life as theirs,
As free from Summer's sultry cares,
And only wishes that his own
Could meet with joys so thickly sown:
Sport seems the all that they pursue,
And play the only work they do.

The cow-boy still cuts short the day,
By mingling mischief with his play;
Oft in the pond, with weeds o'ergrown,
Hurling quick the plashing stone
To cheat his dog, who watching lies,
And instant plunges for the prize;
And though each effort proves in vain,
He shakes his coat, and dives again,
Till, wearied with the fruitless play,

He drops his tail, and sneaks away,
Nor longer heeds the bawling boy,
Who seeks new sports with added joy:
Now on some bank's o'erhanging brow
Beating the wasp's nest with a bough,
Till armies from the hole appear,
And threaten vengeance in his ear
With such determined hue-and-cry
As makes the bold besieger fly;
Then, pelting with excessive glee
The squirrel on the woodland-tree,
Who nimbles round from grain to grain,
And cocks his tail, and peeps again,
Half-pleased, as if he thought the fray
Which mischief made, was meant for play,
Till scared and startled into flight,
He instant tumbles out of sight.
Thus he his leisure hour employs,
And feeds on busy meddling joys,
While in the willow-shaded pool
His cattle stand, their hides to cool.

Loud is the Summer's busy song,
The smallest breeze can find a tongue,
While insects of each tiny size
Grow teazing with their melodies,
Till noon burns with its blistering breath
Around, and day dies still as death.
The busy noise of man and brute
Is on a sudden lost and mute;
Even the brook that leaps along
Seems weary of its bubbling song,
And, so soft its waters creep,
Tired silence sinks in sounder sleep.
The cricket on its banks is dumb,
The very flies forget to hum;

And, save the waggon rocking round,
The landscape sleeps without a sound.
The breeze is stopt, the lazy bough
Hath not a leaf that dances now;
The tottergrass upon the hill,
And spiders' threads, are standing still;
The feathers dropt from moorhen's wing,
Which to the water's surface cling,
Are steadfast, and as heavy seem
As stones beneath them in the stream;
Hawkweed and groundsel's fanning downs
Unruffled keep their seedy crowns;
And in the oven-heated air,
Not one light thing is floating there,
Save that to the earnest eye,
The restless heat seems twittering by.
Noon swoons beneath the heat it made,
And flowers e'en wither in the shade,
Until the sun slopes in the west,
Like weary traveller, glad to rest,
On pillowed clouds of many hues;
Then nature's voice its joy renews,
And chequer'd field and grassy plain
Hum, with their summer songs again,
A requiem to the day's decline,
Whose setting sunbeams coolly shine,
As welcome to day's feeble powers
As falling dews to thirsty flowers.

Now to the pleasant pasture dells,
Where hay from closes sweetly smells,
Adown the pathway's narrow lane
The milking maiden hies again,
With scraps of ballads never dumb,
And rosy cheeks of happy bloom,
Tann'd brown by Summer's rude embrace.

Which adds new beauties to her face,
And red lips never pale with sighs,
And flowing hair, and laughing eyes
That o'er full many a heart prevail'd,
And swelling bosom loosely veiled,
White as the love it harbours there,
Unsullied with the taunts of care.

The mower now gives labour o'er,
And on his bench beside the door
Sits down to see his children play,
Smoking a leisure hour away:
While from her cage the blackbird sings,
That on the woodbine arbour hings;
And all with soothing joys receive
The quiet of a Summer's eve.

NOVEMBER

THE landscape sleeps in mist from morn till noon;
  And, if the sun looks through, 'tis with a face
Beamless and pale and round, as if the moon,
  When done the journey of her nightly race,
Had found him sleeping, and supplied his place.
For days the shepherds in the fields may be,
  Nor mark a patch of sky—blindfold they trace,
The plains, that seem without a bush or tree,
Whistling aloud by guess, to flocks they cannot
    see.

The timid hare seems half its fears to lose,
  Crouching and sleeping 'neath its grassy lair,
And scarcely startles, tho' the shepherd goes
  Close by its home, and dogs are barking there;
The wild colt only turns around to stare
At passer by, then knaps his hide again;

And moody crows beside the road forbear
  To fly, tho' pelted by the passing swain;
Thus day seems turn'd to night, and tries to wake
    in vain.

The owlet leaves her hiding-place at noon,
  And flaps her grey wings in the doubling light;
The hoarse jay screams to see her out so soon,
  And small birds chirp and startle with affright;
  Much doth it scare the superstitious wight,
  Who dreams of sorry luck, and sore dismay;
  While cow-boys think the day a dream of night,
  And oft grow fearful on their lonely way,
Fancying that ghosts may wake, and leave their
    graves by day.

Yet but awhile the slumbering weather flings
  Its murky prison round—then winds wake loud;
With sudden stir the startled forest sings
  Winter's returning song—cloud races cloud,
  And the horizon throws away its shroud,
  Sweeping a stretching circle from the eye;
  Storms upon storms in quick succession crowd,
  And o'er the sameness of the purple sky
Heaven paints, with hurried hand, wild hues of
    every dye.

At length it comes among the forest oaks,
  With sobbing ebbs, and uproar gathering high;
The scared, hoarse raven on its cradle croaks,
  And stockdove-flocks in hurried terrors fly,
  While the blue hawk hangs o'er them in the sky.—
  The hedger hastens from the storm begun,
  To seek a shelter that may keep him dry;
  And foresters low bent, the wind to shun,
Scarce hear amid the strife the poacher's muttering
    gun.

The ploughman hears its humming rage begin,
  And hies for shelter from his naked toil;
  Buttoning his doublet closer to his chin,
  He bends and scampers o'er the elting soil,
  While clouds above him in wild fury boil,
  And winds drive heavily the beating rain;
  He turns his back to catch his breath awhile,
  Then ekes his speed and faces it again,
To seek the shepherd's hut beside the rushy plain.

The boy, that scareth from the spiry wheat
  The melancholy crow—in hurry weaves,
  Beneath an ivied tree, his sheltering seat,
  Of rushy flags and sedges tied in sheaves,
  Or from the field a shock of stubble thieves.
  There he doth dithering sit, and entertain
  His eyes with marking the storm-driven leaves;
  Oft spying nests where he spring eggs had ta'en,
And wishing in his heart 'twas summer-time again.

Thus wears the month along, in checker'd moods,
  Sunshine and shadows, tempests loud, and calms;
  One hour dies silent o'er the sleepy woods,
  The next wakes loud with unexpected storms;
  A dreary nakedness the field deforms—
  Yet many a rural sound, and rural sight,
  Lives in the village still about the farms,
  Where toil's rude uproar hums from morn till night
Noises, in which the ears of Industry delight.

At length the stir of rural labour's still,
  And Industry her care awhile foregoes;
  When Winter comes in earnest to fulfil
  His yearly task, at bleak November's close,

And stops the plough, and hides the field in
    snows;
When frost locks up the stream in chill delay,
And mellows on the hedge the jetty sloes,
For little birds—then Toil hath time for play,
And nought but threshers' flails awake the dreary
    day.

LIFE, DEATH, AND ETERNITY

A SHADOW moving by one's side,
    That would a substance seem,—
That is, yet is not,—though descried—
    Like skies beneath the stream;
A tree that's ever in the bloom,
    Whose fruit is never rife;
A wish for joys that never come,—
    Such are the hopes of Life.

A dark, inevitable night,
    A blank that will remain;
A waiting for the morning light,
    Where waiting is in vain;
A gulph, where pathway never led
    To show the depth beneath;
A thing we know not, yet we dread,—
    That dreaded thing is Death.

The vaulted void of purple sky
    That every where extends,
That stretches from the dazzled eye,
    In space that never ends;
A morning whose uprisen sun
    No setting e'er shall see;
A day that comes without a noon,—
    Such is Eternity.

AUTUMN

Syren of sullen moods and fading hues,
Yet haply not incapable of joy,
　　Sweet Autumn! I thee hail
　　With welcome all unfeigned;

And oft as morning from her lattice peeps
To beckon up the sun, I seek with thee
　　To drink the dewy breath
　　Of fields left fragrant then,

In solitudes, where no frequented paths
But what thy own foot makes betray thine home,
　　Stealing obtrusive there
　　To meditate thy end:

By overshadowed ponds, in woody nooks,
With ramping sallows lined, and crowding sedge,
　　Which woo the winds to play,
　　And with them dance for joy;

And meadow pools, torn wide by lawless floods,
Where water-lilies spread their oily leaves,
　　On which, as wont, the fly
　　Oft battens in the sun;

Where leans the mossy willow half way o'er,
On which the shepherd crawls astride to throw
　　His angle, clear of weeds
　　That crowd the water's brim;

Or crispy hills, and hollows scant of sward,
Where step by step the patient lonely boy,
　　Hath cut rude flights of stairs
　　To climb their steepy sides;

Then track along their feet, grown hoarse with noise,
The crawling brook, that ekes its weary speed,
　　And struggles through the weeds
　　With faint and sullen brawl.—

These haunts I long have favoured, more as now
With thee thus wandering, moralizing on,
    Stealing glad thoughts from grief,
    And happy, though I sigh.

Sweet Vision, with the wild dishevelled hair,
And raiment shadowy of each wind's embrace,
    Fain would I win thine harp
    To one accordant theme.

Now not inaptly craved, communing thus,
Beneath the curdled arms of this stunt oak,
    While pillowed on the grass,
    We fondly ruminate

O'er the disordered scenes of woods and fields,
Ploughed lands, thin travelled with half-hungry sheep,
    Pastures tracked deep with cows,
    Where small birds seek for seed:

Marking the cow-boy that so merry trills
His frequent, unpremeditated song,
    Wooing the winds to pause,
    Till echo brawls again;

As on with plashy step, and clouted shoon,
He roves, half indolent and self-employed,
    To rob the little birds
    Of hips and pendant haws,

And sloes, dim covered as with dewy veils,
And rambling bramble-berries, pulpy and sweet,
    Arching their prickly trails
    Half o'er the narrow lane:

Noting the hedger front with stubborn face
The dank bleak wind, that whistles thinly by
    His leathern garb, thorn proof,
    And cheek red hot with toil;

While o'er the pleachy lands of mellow brown,
The mower's stubbling scythe clogs to his foot
    The ever eking whisp,
    With sharp and sudden jerk,

Till into formal rows the russet shocks
Crowd the blank field to thatch time-weathered barns,
    And hovels rude repair,
    Stript by disturbing winds.

See! from the rustling scythe the haunted hare
Scampers circuitous, with startled ears
    Prickt up, then squat, as by
    She brushes to the woods,

Where reeded grass, breast-high and undisturbed,
Forms pleasant clumps, through which the soothing
       winds
    Soften her rigid fears,
    And lull to calm repose.

Wild Sorceress! me thy restless mood delights,
More than the stir of summer's crowded scenes,
    Where, jostled in the din,
    Joy palled my ear with song;

Heart-sickening for the silence, that is here
Not broken inharmoniously, as now
    That lone and vagrant bee
    Booms faint with weary chime.

Now filtering winds thin winnow through the woods
In tremulous noise, that bids, at every breath,
    Some sickly cankered leaf
    Let go its hold, and die.

And now the bickering storm, with sudden start,
In flirting fits of anger carps aloud,
    Thee urging to thine end,
    Sore wept by troubled skies.

And yet, sublime in grief! thy thoughts delight
To show me visions of most gorgeous dyes,
    Haply forgetting now
    They but prepare thy shroud;

Thy pencil dashing its excess of shades,
Improvident of waste, till every bough
    Burns with thy mellow touch
    Disorderly divine.

Soon must I view thee as a pleasant dream
Droop faintly, and so reckon for thine end,
    As sad the winds sink low
    In dirges for their queen;

While in the moment of their weary pause,
To cheer thy bankrupt pomp, the willing lark
    Starts from his shielding clod,
    Snatching sweet scraps of song.

Thy life is waning now, and Silence tries
To mourn, but meets no sympathy in sounds,
    As stooping low she bends,
    Forming with leaves thy grave;

To sleep inglorious there mid tangled woods,
Till parched lipped Summer pines in drought away.
    Then from thine ivy'd trance
    Awake to glories new.

SUMMER IMAGES

Now swarthy Summer, by rude health embrowned,
  Precedence takes of rosy fingered Spring ;
And laughing Joy, with wild flowers prank'd, and
      crown'd,
  A wild and giddy thing,
And Health robust, from every care unbound,
  Come on the zephyr's wing,
    And cheer the toiling clown.

Happy as holiday-enjoying face,
  Loud tongued, and 'merry as a marriage bell,'
Thy lightsome step sheds joy in every place ;
  And where the troubled dwell,
Thy witching charms wean them of half their cares ;
  And from thy sunny spell,
    They greet joy unawares.

Then with thy sultry locks all loose and rude,
  And mantle laced with gems of garish light,
Come as of wont ; for I would fain intrude,
  And in the world's despite,
Share the rude wealth that thy own heart beguiles ;
  If haply so I might
    Win pleasure from thy smiles.

Me not the noise of brawling pleasure cheers,
  In nightly revels or in city streets ;
But joys which soothe, and not distract the ears,
  That one at leisure meets
In the green woods, and meadows summer-shorn,
  Or fields, where bee-fly greets
    The ear with mellow horn.

The green-swathed grasshopper, on treble pipe,
  Sings there, and dances, in mad-hearted pranks;
There bees go courting every flower that 's ripe,
  On baulks and sunny banks;
And droning dragon-fly, on rude bassoon,
   Attempts to give God thanks
     In no discordant tune.

The speckled thrush, by self-delight embued,
  There sings unto himself for joy's amends,
And drinks the honey dew of solitude.
  There Happiness attends
With inbred Joy until the heart o'erflow,
   Of which the world's rude friends,
     Nought heeding, nothing know.

There the gay river, laughing as it goes,
  Plashes with easy wave its flaggy sides,
And to the calm of heart, in calmness shows
  What pleasure there abides,
To trace its sedgy banks, from trouble free:
   Spots, Solitude provides
     To muse, and happy be.

There ruminating 'neath some pleasant bush,
  On sweet silk grass I stretch me at mine ease,
Where I can pillow on the yielding rush;
  And, acting as I please,
Drop into pleasant dreams; or musing lie,
   Mark the wind-shaken trees,
     And cloud-betravelled sky.

There think me how some barter joy for care,
  And waste life's summer-health in riot rude,
Of nature, nor of nature's sweets aware.
  When passions vain intrude,
These, by calm musings, softened are and still;
  And the heart's better mood
      Feels sick of doing ill.

There I can live, and at my leisure seek
  Joys far from cold restraints—not fearing pride—
Free as the winds, that breathe upon my cheek
  Rude health, so long denied.
Here poor Integrity can sit at ease,
  And list self-satisfied
      The song of honey-bees;

The green lane now I traverse, where it goes
  Nought guessing, till some sudden turn espies
Rude batter'd finger post, that stooping shows
  Where the snug mystery lies;
And then a mossy spire, with ivy crown,
  Cheers up the short surprise,
      And shows a peeping town.

I see the wild flowers, in their summer morn
  Of beauty, feeding on joy's luscious hours;
The gay convolvulus, wreathing round the thorn,
  Agape for honey showers;
And slender kingcup, burnished with the dew
  Of morning's early hours,
      Like gold yminted new.

And mark by rustic bridge, o'er shallow stream,
  Cow-tending boy, to toil unreconciled,
Absorbed as in some vagrant summer dream;
  Who now, in gestures wild,
Starts dancing to his shadow on the wall,
  Feeling self-gratified,
      Nor fearing human thrall.

Or thread the sunny valley laced with streams,
  Or forests rude, and the o'ershadow'd brims
Of simple ponds, where idle shepherd dreams,
  Stretching his listless limbs;
Or trace hay-scented meadows, smooth and long,
  Where joy's wild impulse swims
      In one continued song.

I love at early morn, from new mown swath,
  To see the startled frog his route pursue;
To mark while, leaping o'er the dripping path,
  His bright sides scatter dew,
The early lark that, from its bustle flies,
  To hail his matin new;
      And watch him to the skies.

To note on hedgerow baulks, in moisture sprent,
  The jetty snail creep from the mossy thorn,
With earnest heed, and tremulous intent,
  Frail brother of the morn,
That from the tiny bent's dew-misted leaves
  Withdraws his timid horn,
      And fearful vision weaves.

Or swallow heed on smoke-tanned chimney top,
   Wont to be first unsealing Morning's eye,
Ere yet the bee hath gleaned one wayward drop
   Of honey on his thigh;
To see him seek morn's airy couch to sing,
   Until the golden sky
      Bepaint his russet wing.

Or sauntering boy by tanning corn to spy,
   With clapping noise to startle birds away,
And hear him bawl to every passer by
   To know the hour of day;
While the uncradled breezes, fresh and strong,
   With waking blossoms play,
      And breathe Æolian song.

I love the south-west wind, or low or loud,
   And not the less when sudden drops of rain
Moisten my glowing cheek from ebon cloud,
   Threatening soft showers again,
That over lands new ploughed and meadow grounds,
   Summer's sweet breath unchain,
      And wake harmonious sounds.

Rich music breathes in Summer's every sound;
   And in her harmony of varied greens,
Woods, meadows, hedge-rows, corn-fields, all around
   Much beauty intervenes,
Filling with harmony the ear and eye;
   While o'er the mingling scenes
      Far spreads the laughing sky.

See, how the wind-enamoured aspen leaves
  Turn up their silver lining to the sun!
And hark! the rustling noise, that oft deceives,
  And makes the sheep-boy run:
The sound so mimics fast-approaching showers,
  He thinks the rain's begun,
      And hastes to sheltering bowers.

But now the evening curdles dank and grey,
  Changing her watchet hue for sombre weed;
And moping owls, to close the lids of day,
  On drowsy wing proceed;
While chickering crickets, tremulous and long,
  Light's farewell inly heed,
      And give it parting song.

The pranking bat its flighty circlet makes;
  The glow-worm burnishes its lamp anew;
O'er meadows dew-besprent, the beetle wakes
  Inquiries ever new,
Teazing each passing ear with murmurs vain,
  As wanting to pursue
      His homeward path again.

Hark! 'tis the melody of distant bells
  That on the wind with pleasing hum rebounds
By fitful starts, then musically swells
  O'er the dim stilly grounds;
While on the meadow-bridge the pausing boy
  Listens the mellow sounds,
      And hums in vacant joy.

Now homeward-bound, the hedger bundles round
  His evening faggot, and with every stride
His leathern doublet leaves a rustling sound,
  Till silly sheep beside
His path start tremulous, and once again
  Look back dissatisfied,
      And scour the dewy plain.

How sweet the soothing calmness that distills
  O'er the heart's every sense its opiate dews,
In meek-eyed moods and ever balmy trills!
  That softens and subdues,
With gentle Quiet's bland and sober train,
  Which dreamy eve renews
      In many a mellow strain!

I love to walk the fields, they are to me
  A legacy no evil can destroy;
They, like a spell, set every rapture free
  That cheer'd me when a boy.
Play—pastime—all Time's blotting pen conceal'd,
  Comes like a new-born joy,
      To greet me in the field.

For Nature's objects ever harmonize
  With emulous Taste, that vulgar deed annoys;
Which loves in pensive moods to sympathize,
  And meet vibrating joys
O'er Nature's pleasing things; nor slighting, deems
  Pastimes, the Muse employs,
      Vain and obtrusive themes.

INSECTS

THESE tiny loiterers on the barley's beard,
And happy units of a numerous herd
Of playfellows, the laughing Summer brings,
Mocking the sunshine on their glittering wings,
How merrily they creep, and run, and fly!
No kin they bear to labour's drudgery,
Smoothing the velvet of the pale hedge-rose;
And where they fly for dinner no one knows—
The dew-drops feed them not—they love the shine
Of noon, whose suns may bring them golden wine
All day they're playing in their Sunday dress—
When night reposes, for they can do no less;
Then, to the heath-bell's purple hood they fly,
And like to princes in their slumbers lie,
Secure from rain, and dropping dews, and all,
In silken beds and roomy painted hall.
So merrily they spend their summer-day,
Now in the corn-fields, now the new-mown hay.
One almost fancies that such happy things,
With coloured hoods and richly burnished wings,
Are fairy folk, in splendid masquerade
Disguised, as if of mortal folk afraid,
Keeping their joyous pranks a mystery still,
Lest glaring day should do their secrets ill.

CLARE   H

SUDDEN SHOWER

BLACK grows the southern sky, betokening rain,
  And humming hive-bees homeward hurry by:
They feel the change; so let us shun the grain,
  And take the broad road while our feet are dry.
Aye there, some drops fell moistening on my face,
  And pattering on my hat—'tis coming nigh!—
Let's look about, and find a sheltering place.
  The little things around us fear the sky,
And hasten through the grass to shun the shower.
  Here stoops an ash-tree—hark! the wind gets high,
But never mind; this ivy, for an hour,
  Rain as it may, will keep us drily here:
That little wren knows well his sheltering bower,
  Nor leaves his covert, though we come so near.

BEANS IN BLOSSOM

THE south-west wind! how pleasant in the face
It breathes! while, sauntering in a musing pace,
I roam these new ploughed fields; or by the side
Of this old wood, where happy birds abide,
And the rich blackbird, through his golden bill,
Utters wild music when the rest are still.
Luscious the scent comes of the blossomed bean,
As o'er the path in rich disorder lean
Its stalks; whence bees, in busy rows and toils,
Load home luxuriantly their yellow spoils.
The herd-cows toss the molehills in their play;
And often stand the stranger's steps at bay,
Mid clover blossoms red and tawny white,
Strong scented with the summer's warm delight.

EVENING PRIMROSE

When once the sun sinks in the west,
And dew-drops pearl the Evening's breast;
Almost as pale as moonbeams are,
Or its companionable star,
The Evening Primrose opes anew
Its delicate blossoms to the dew;
And hermit-like, shunning the light,
Wastes its fair bloom upon the Night;
Who, blindfold to its fond caresses,
Knows not the beauty he possesses.
Thus it blooms on while Night is by;
When Day looks out with open eye,
'Bashed at the gaze it cannot shun,
It faints, and withers, and is gone.

THE SHEPHERD'S TREE

Huge elm, with rifted trunk all notched and scarred,
   Like to a warrior's destiny! I love
To stretch me often on thy shadowed sward,
   And hear the laugh of summer leaves above;
Or on thy buttressed roots to sit, and lean
   In careless attitude, and there reflect
On times, and deeds, and darings that have been—
   Old castaways, now swallowed in neglect;
While thou art towering in thy strength of heart,
   Stirring the soul to vain imaginings,
In which life's sordid being hath no part.
   The wind of that eternal ditty sings
Humming of future things, that burn the mind
To leave some fragment of itself behind.

NUTTING

THE Sun had stooped, his westward clouds to win,
Like weary traveller seeking for an inn;
When from the hazelly wood we glad descried
The ivied gateway by the pasture side.
Long had we sought for nuts amid the shade,
Where Silence fled the rustle that we made;
When torn by briars, and brushed by sedges rank,
We left the wood, and on the velvet bank
Of short sward pasture-ground we sat us down,
To shell our nuts before we reached the town.
The near-hand stubble-field, with mellow glower,
Showed the dimmed blaze of poppies still in flower;
And sweet the mole-hills were we sat upon—
Again the thyme's in bloom, but where is Pleasure
      gone?

DEATH OF BEAUTY

Now thou art gone, the fairy rose is fled,
  That erst gay Fancy's garden did adorn.
Thine was the dew on which her folly fed,
  The sun by which she glittered in the morn.
Now thou art gone, her pride is withered;
  In dress of common weeds she doth array,
And vanity neglects her in its play.
  Thou wert the very index of her praise,
Her borrowed bloom was kindled from thy rays;
  Like dancing insects that the sun allures,
She little heeded it was gained from thee.
  Vain joys! what are they now their sun's away?
What! but poor shadows, that blank night obscures,
  As the grave hides what would dishonoured be.

DECAY

Amidst the happiest joy, a shade of grief
Will come;—its mark, in summer time, a leaf,
Tinged with the Autumn's visible decay,
As pining to forgetfulness away,—
Aye, blank Forgetfulness!—that coldest lot,
To be,—and to have been,—and then be not.
E'en Beauty's self, love's essence, heaven's prime,
Meet for eternity in joys sublime,
Earth's most divinest,—is a mortal thing,
And nurses Time's sick Autumn for its Spring;
And fades, and fades, till Wonder knows it not,
And Admiration hath all praise forgot;
Coldly forsaking an unheeding past,
To fade, and fall, and die, like common things at
     last.

THE FLITTING

I've left my own old home of homes,
Green fields and every pleasant place;
The summer like a stranger comes,
I pause and hardly know her face.
I miss the hazel's happy green,
The blue bell's quiet hanging blooms,
Where envy's sneer was never seen,
Where staring malice never comes.

I miss the heath, its yellow furze,
Molehills and rabbit tracks that lead
Through beesom, ling, and teazel burrs
That spread a wilderness indeed;
The woodland oaks and all below
That their white powdered branches shield,
The mossy paths: the very crow
Croaked music in my native fields.

I sit me in my corner chair
That seems to feel itself at home,
And hear bird music here and there
From hawthorn hedge and orchard come;
I hear, but all is strange and new:
I sat on my old bench in June,
The sailing puddock's shrill 'peelew'
On Royce Wood seemed a sweeter tune.

I walk adown the narrow lane,
The nightingale is singing now,
But like to me she seems at loss
For Royce Wood and its shielding bough.
I lean upon the window sill,
The bees and summer happy seem;
Green, sunny green they shine, but still
My heart goes far away to dream

Of happiness, and thoughts arise
With home-bred pictures many a one,
Green lanes that shut out burning skies
And old crook'd stiles to rest upon;
Above them hangs the maple tree,
Below grass swells a velvet hill,
And little footpaths sweet to see
Go seeking sweeter places still.

With bye and bye a brook to cross
O'er which a little arch is thrown:
No brook is here, I feel the loss
From home and friends and all alone.
— The stone pit with its shelvy sides
Seemed hanging rocks in my esteem;
I miss the prospect far and wide
From Langley bush, and so I seem

Alone and in a stranger scene,'
Far, far from spots my heart esteems,
The closen with their ancient green,
Heaths, woods, and pastures, sunny streams.
The hawthorns here were hung with may
But still they seem in deader green,
The sun e'en seems to loose its way
Nor knows the quarter it is in.

I dwell in trifles like a child,
I feel as ill becomes a man,
And still my thoughts like weedlings wild
Grow up to blossom where they can.
They turn to places known so long
I feel that joy was dwelling there,
So homebred pleasure fills the song
That has no present joys to hear.

I read in books for happiness,
But books mistake the way to joy,
They change as well: give age the glass
To hunt its visage when a boy.
For books they follow fashions new
And throw all old esteems away,
In crowded streets flowers never grew,
But many there hath died away.

Some sing the pomps of chivalry
As legends of the ancient time,
Where gold and pearls and mystery
Are shadows painted for sublime;
But passions of sublimity
Belong to plain and simpler things,
And David underneath a tree
Sought when a shepherd Salem's springs,

Where moss did into cushions spring,
Forming a seat of velvet hue,
A small unnoticed trifling thing
To all but heaven's daily dew.
And David's crown hath passed away,
Yet poesy breaths his shepherd-skill,
His palace lost, and to this day
The little moss is blossoming still.

Strange scenes mere shadows are to me,
Vague impersonifying things;
I love with my old haunts to be
By quiet roads and gravel springs,
Where little pebbles wear as smooth
As hermits' beads by gentle floods,
Whose noises do my spirits soothe
And warm them into singing moods.

Here every tree is strange to me,
All foreign things where'er I go,
There's none where boyhood made a [   ]¹
Or clambered up to rob a crow.
No hollow tree or woodland bower
Well known when joy was beating high,
Where beauty ran to shun a shower
And love took pains to keep her dry,

And laid the sheaf upon the ground
To keep her from the dripping grass,
And ran for stooks and set them round
Till scarce a drop of rain could pass
Through; where the maidens they reclined
And sung sweet ballads now forgot,
Which brought sweet memories to the mind,
But here a memory knows them not.

¹ This word is illegible.

There have I sat by many a tree
And leaned o'er many a rural stile,
And conned my thoughts as joys to me,
Nought heeding who might frown or smile.
'Twas nature's beauties that inspired
My heart with rapture not its own,
And she's a fay that never tires;
How could I feel myself alone?

No, pasture molehills used to lie
And talk to me of sunny days,
And then the glad sheep resting by
All still in ruminating praise
Of summer and the pleasant place
And every weed and blossom too
Was looking upward in my face
With friendship's welcome 'how do ye do?'

All tenants of an ancient place
And heirs of noble heritage,
Coeval they with Adam's race
And blest with more substantial age.
For when the world first saw the sun
These little flowers beheld him too,
And when his love for earth begun
They were the first his smiles to woo.

There little lambtoe bunches springs
In red tinged and begolden dye,
For ever, and like China kings
They come but never seem to die.
There may-bloom with its little threads
Still comes upon the thorny bowers
And ne'er forgets those pinky heads
Like fairy pins amid the flowers.

And still they bloom as on the day
They first crowned wilderness and rock,
When Abel haply crowned with may
The firstlings of his little flock,
And Eve sought from the matted thorn
To deck her lone and lovely brow
With that same rose that heedless scorn
Misnames as the dog rosey now.

Give me no high-flown fangled things,
No haughty pomp in marching chime,
Where Muses play on golden strings
And splendour passes for sublime,
Where cities stretch as far as fame
And fancy's sharing eye can go,
And piled until the sky for shame
Is stooping far away below.

I love the verse that mild and bland
Breathes of green fields and open sky,
I love the Muse that in her hand
Bears wreaths of native poesy.
Who walks nor skips the pasture brook
In scorn, but by the drinking horse
Leans o'er its little brig to look
How far the sallows lean across,

And feels a rapture in her breast
Upon their root-fringed [   ]¹ to mark
A hermit morehen's sedgy nest
Just like a naiad's summer bark.
She counts the eggs she cannot reach
Admires the spot and loves it well,
And yearns, so nature's lessons teach,
Amid such neighbourhoods to dwell.

¹ This word is illegible.

I love the Muse who sits her down
Upon the molehill's little lap,
Who feels no fear to stain her gown
And pauses by the hedgerow gap;
Not with that affectation, praise
Of song to sing, and never see
A field flower grown in all her days
Or e'en a forest's aged tree.

E'en here my simple feelings nurse
A love for every simple weed,
And e'en this little shepherd's purse
Grieves me to cut it up; indeed
I feel at times a love and joy
For every weed and every thing,
A feeling kindred from a boy,
A feeling brought with every Spring.

And why? this 'shepherd's purse' that grows
In this strange spot in days gone bye
Grew in the little garden rows
Of that old hut now left; and I
Feel what I never felt before,
This weed an ancient neighbour here,
And though I own the spot no more
Its every trifle makes it dear.

The ivy at the parlour end,
The woodbine at the garden gate,
Are all and each affection's friend
That renders parting desolate.
But times will change and friends must part
And nature still can make amends,
Then memory lingers round the heart
Like life whose essence is its friends.

Time looks on pomp with careless moods
Or killing apathy's disdain;
So where old marble cities stood
Poor persecuted weeds remain.
She feels a love for little things
That very few can feel beside,
And still the grass eternal springs
Where castles stood and grandeur died.

REMEMBRANCES

Summer's pleasures they are gone like to visions
    every one,
And the cloudy days of autumn and of winter
    cometh on.
I tried to call them back, but unbidden they are
    gone
Far away from heart and eye and forever far away.
Dear heart, and can it be that such raptures
    meet decay?
I thought them all eternal when by Langley Bush
    I lay,
I thought them joys eternal when I used to shout
    and play
On its bank at clink and bandy chock and law
    and ducking stone,
Where silence sitteth now on the wild heath as
    her own
Like a ruin of the past all alone.

When I used to lie and sing by old Eastwell's
    boiling spring,
When I used to tie the willow boughs together
    for a swing,

And fish with crooked pins and thread and never
  catch a thing,
With heart just like a feather, now as heavy as a
  stone ;
When beneath old Lee Close oak I the bottom
  branches broke
To make our harvest cart like so many working folk,
And then to cut a straw at the brook to have a soak.
O I never dreamed of parting or that trouble had
  a sting,
Or that pleasures like a flock of birds would ever
  take to wing,
Leaving nothing but a little naked spring.

When jumping time away on old Crossberry way,
And eating awes like sugarplums ere they had lost
  the may,
And skipping like a leveret before the peep of day
On the roly poly up and downs of pleasant
  Swordy Well,
When in Round Oak's narrow lane as the south
  got black again
We sought the hollow ash that was shelter from
  the rain,
With our pockets full of peas we had stolen from
  the grain ;
How delicious was the dinner time on such a
  showery day !
O words are poor receipts for what time hath stole
  away,
The ancient pulpit trees and the play.

When for school o'er little field with its brook
  and wooden brig,
Where I swaggered like a man though I was not
  half so big,

While I held my little plough though 'twas but a
    willow twig,
And drove my team along made of nothing but a
    name,
'Gee hep' and 'hoit' and 'woi'—O I never call
    to mind
Those pleasant names of places but I leave a sigh
    behind,
While I see little mouldiwarps hang sweeing to the
    the wind
On the only aged willow that in all the field
    remains,
And nature hides her face while they're sweeing
    in their chains
And in a silent murmuring complains.

Here was commons for their hills where they seek
    for freedom still,
Though every common's gone and though traps
    are set to kill
The little homeless miners—O it turns my bosom
    chill
When I think of old Sneap Green, Puddock's Nook
    and Hilly Snow,
Where bramble bushes grew and the daisy gemmed
    in dew
And the hills of silken grass like to cushions to
    the view,
Where we threw the pismire crumbs when we'd
    nothing else to do,
All levelled like a desert by the never weary
    plough,
All banished like the sun where that cloud is
    passing now
And settled here for ever on its brow.

O I never thought that joys would run away from
    boys,
Or that boys should change their minds and forsake
    such summer joys;
But alack I never dreamed that the world had
    other toys
To petrify first feelings like the fable into stone,
Till I found the pleasure past and a winter come
    at last,
Then the fields were sudden bare and the sky got
    overcast
And boyhood's pleasing haunt like a blossom in the
    blast
Was shrivelled to a withered weed and trampled
    down and done,
Till vanished was the morning spring and set the
    summer sun
And winter fought her battle strife and won.

By Langley Bush I roam but the bush hath left
    its hill,
On Cowper Green I stray, 'tis a desert strange and
    chill,
And spreading Lee Close oak, ere decay had penned
    its will,
To the axe of the spoiler and self-interest fell a prey,
And Crossberry Way and old Round Oak's narrow
    lane
With its hollow trees like pulpits I shall never see
    again.
Enclosure like a Buonaparte let not a thing remain,
It levelled every bush and tree and levelled every
    hill
And hung the moles for traitors, though the brook
    is running still
It runs a naked stream cold and chill.

O had I known as then joy had left the paths of
    men,
I had watched her night and day, be sure, and never
    slept again,
And when she turned to go, O I'd caught her
    mantle then,
And wooed her like a lover by my lonely side to
    stay;
Ay, knelt and worshipped on, as love in beauty's
    bower,
And clung upon her smiles as a bee upon a flower,
And gave her heart my poesies, all cropt in a sunny,
    hour,
As keepsakes and pledges all to never fade away;
But love never heeded to treasure up the may,
So it went the common road to decay.

EXPECTATION: A BALLAD

'Tis Saturday night and my shepherd will come
With a hallo and whistle for me;
Be clear, O ye skies, take your storm further home,
Let no rain drench our favourite tree.
For I fear by the things that are hopping about
There's a sign of a storm coming on;
The frog looks as black as the toad that creeps out
From under its hiding stone.

The cat with her tail runneth round till she reels
And the pigs race with mouthfuls of hay;
I sigh at the sight: I felt sick over meals,
For I'm lone when my shepherd's away.
When dogs eat the grass it is sure to be rain,
And our dogs in the orchard do now;
The swallows fly low and my heart is in pain
While the flies even madden the cow.

The pigeons have moped on the cote the day long
And the hens went to roost before noon;
The blackbirds, long still, din the woods with their
      song
And they look upon showers as a boon,
While they keep their nest dry in the wet hazel
      bush
And moisten their black sooty wings;
Did they know but my sorrows they'd quickly be
      hush:
Birds to make lovers happy should sing.

I've often leaned over the croft's mossy gate
To listen birds singing at night,
When I for the sure-footed Rover did wait,
And rich was my bosom's delight.
And sweet had it been now I'm waiting anew
Till the black snail is out from the grain,
But the south's ruddy clouds they have turned black
      and blue
And the blackbirds are singing for rain.

The Thrush 'wivy wit wivy wit' t'other night
Sung aloud in the old sallow bush,
And I called him a pert little urchin outright
To sing 'heavy wet'; and the thrush
Changed his note in a moment to 'Cheer up' and
      'cheer'
And the clouds crept away from the sun,
Till my shepherd he came, and when thrushes I hear
My heart with the music is won.

But the blackbird is rude and insulting, and now,
The more the clouds blacken the sky,
The louder he sings from the green hazel bough,
But he may be sad bye and bye.

For the cow boy is stopping beneath the oak tree
Whose branches hang down to the ground,
And beating his stick on the bushes to see
If a bird startles out from the sound.

So silence is safety, and, bird, have a care
Or your song will your dwelling betray,
For yesterday morning I saw your nest there
But sung not to fright ye away.
And now the boy's near you: well done, cunning
        bird,
You have ceased and popt out t'other side;
Your nest it is safe, not a leaf has he stirred,
And I have my shepherd descried.

THE TOPER'S RANT

COME, come, my old crones and gay fellows
That love to drink ale in a horn,
We'll sing racy songs now we're mellow
Which topers sung ere we were born.
For our bottle kind fate shall be thanked,
And line but our pockets with brass,
We'll sooner suck ale through a blanket
Than thimbles of wine from a glass.

Away with your proud thimble glasses
Of wine foreign nations supply,
We topers ne'er drink to the lasses
Over draughts scarce enough for a fly.
Club us with the hedger and ditcher
Or beggar that makes his own horn,
To join us o'er bottle or pitcher
Foaming o'er with the essence of corn.

We care not with whom we get tipsy
Or where with brown stout we regale,
We'll weather the storm with a gipsy
If he be a lover of ale.
We'll weather the toughest storm weary
Although we get wet to the skin,
If outside our cottage looks dreary
We're warm and right happy within.

We'll sit till the bushes are dropping
Like the spout of a watering pan,
For till the dram's drank there's no stopping,
We'll keep up the ring to a man.
We'll sit till dame nature is feeling
The breath of our stingo so warm,
And bushes and trees begin reeling
In our eyes like to ships in a storm.

We'll sit for three hours before seven,
When larks wake the morning to dance,
Till night's sooty brood of eleven,
When witches ride over to France.
We'll sit it in spite of the weather
Till we tumble our length on the plain,
When the morning shall find us together
To play the game over again.

THE COTTAGER

TRUE as the church clock hand the hour pursues
He plods about his toils and reads the news,
And at the blacksmith's shop his hour will stand
To talk of 'Lunun' as a foreign land.
For from his cottage door in peace or strife
He ne'er went fifty miles in all his life.

His knowledge with old notions still combined
Is twenty years behind the march of mind.
He views new knowledge with suspicious eyes
And thinks it blasphemy to be so wise.
On steam's almighty tales he wondering looks
As witchcraft gleaned from old black letter books.
Life gave him comfort but denied him wealth,
He toils in quiet and enjoys his health.
He smokes a pipe at night and drinks his beer
And runs no scores on tavern screens to clear.
He goes to market all the year about
And keeps one hour and never stays it out.
E'en at St. Thomas tide old Rover's bark
Hails Dapple's trot an hour before it's dark.
He is a simple-worded plain old man
Whose good intents take errors in their plan.
Oft sentimental and with saddened vein
He looks on trifles and bemoans their pain,
And thinks the angler mad, and loudly storms
With emphasis of speech o'er murdered worms.
O hunters cruel! pleading with sad care
Pity's petition for the fox and hare,
Yet feels self-satisfaction in his woes
For war's crushed myriads of his slaughtered foes.
He is right scrupulous in one pretext
And wholesale errors swallows in the next.
He deems it sin to sing, and yet to say
A song a mighty difference in his way.
And many a moving tale in antique rhymes
He has for Christmas and such merry times,
When 'Chevy Chase', his master piece of song,
Is said so earnest none can think it long.
'Twas the old vicar's way who should be right,
For the old vicar was his heart's delight,
And while at church he often shakes his head
To think what sermons the old vicar made,

Downright and orthodox that all the land
Who had their ears to hear might understand,
But now such mighty learning meets his ears
He thinks it Greek or Latin which he hears,
Yet church receives him every sabbath day
And rain or snow he never keeps away.
All words of reverence still his heart reveres,
Low bows his head when Jesus' name he hears,
And still he thinks it blasphemy as well
Such names without a capital to spell.
In an old corner cupboard by the wall
His books are laid, though good, in number small,
His Bible first in place; from worth and age
Whose grandsire's name adorns the title page,
And blank leaves once, now filled with kindred
    claims,
Displayed a world's epitome of names.
Parents and children and grandchildren all
Memory's affections in the lists recall.
And prayer book next, much worn though strongly
    bound,
Proves him a churchman orthodox and sound.
The 'Pilgrim's Progress' and the 'Death of Abel'
Are seldom missing from his Sunday table,
And prime old Tusser in his homely trim,
The first of bards in all the world with him,
And only Poet which his leisure knows:
Verse deals in fiction, so he sticks to prose.
These are the books he reads and reads again
And weekly hunts the almanacks for rain.
Here and no further learning's channels ran;
Still, neighbours prize him as the learned man.
His cottage is a humble place of rest
With one spare room to welcome every guest,
And that tall poplar pointing to the sky
His own hand planted while an idle boy,

It shades his chimney while the singing wind
Hums songs of shelter to his happy mind.
Within his cot the largest ears of corn
He ever found his picture frames adorn:
Brave Granby's head, De Grosse's grand defeat;
He rubs his hands and shows how Rodney beat.
And from the rafters upon strings depend
Bean stalks beset with pods from end to end,
Whose numbers without counting may be seen
Wrote on the almanack behind the screen.
Around the corner upon worsted strung
Pooties in wreaths above the cupboard hung.
Memory at trifling incidents awakes
And there he keeps them for his children's sakes,
Who when as boys searched every sedgy lane,
Traced every wood and shattered clothes again,
Roaming about on rapture's easy wing
To hunt those very pooty shells in Spring.
And thus he lives too happy to be poor
While strife ne'er pauses at so mean a door.
Low in the sheltered valley stands his cot,
He hears the mountain storm and feels it not;
Winter and spring, toil ceasing ere 'tis dark,
Rests with the lamb and rises with the lark.
Content is helpmate to the day's employ
And care ne'er comes to steal a single joy.
Time, scarcely noticed, turns his hair to grey,
Yet leaves him happy as a child at play.

SHADOWS OF TASTE

Taste with as many hues doth hearts engage
As leaves and flowers do upon nature's page,
Not mind alone the instinctive mood declares
But buds and flowers and insects are its heirs.

Taste is their joyous heritage and they
All choose for joy in a peculiar way;
Buds own it in the various spots they chuse,
Some live content in low grass gemmed with dews,
The yellowhammer like a tasteful guest
'Neath picturesque green molehills makes a nest,
Where oft the shepherd with unlearned ken
Finds strange eggs scribbled as with ink and pen:
He looks with wonder on the learned marks
And calls them in his memory writing larks.
Birds bolder winged on bushes love to be
While some choose cradles on the highest tree,
There rocked by winds they feel no moods of fear
But joy their birthright lives forever near,
And the bold eagle, which man's fear enshrouds,
Would, could he lodge it, house upon the clouds,
While little wrens mistrusting none that come
In each low hovel meet a sheltered home.
Flowers in the wisdom of creative choice
Seem blest with feeling and a silent voice;
Some on the barren roads delight to bloom
And others haunt the melancholy tomb
Where Death, the blight of all, finds summer's hours
Too kind to miss him with her host of flowers.
Some flourish in the sun and some the shade,
Who almost in his morning smiles would fade
These in leaf-darkened woods right timid stray
And in its green night smile their lives away.
Others in water live and scarcely seem
To peep their little flowers above the stream,
While water lilies in their glories come
And spread green isles of beauty round their home.
All share the summer's glory and its good
And taste of joy in each peculiar mood;
Insects of varied taste in rapture share
The heyday luxuries which she comes to heir,

In wild disorder various routs they run,
In water, earth, still shade, and busy sun,
And in the crowd of green earth's busy claims
They e'en grow nameless 'mid so many names.
And man, that noble insect, restless man,
Whose thoughts scale heaven in its mighty span,
Pours forth his living soul in many a shade
And taste runs riot in her every grade.
While the low herd, mere savages subdued,
With nought of feeling or of taste imbued,
Pass over sweetest scenes a careless eye
As blank as midnight in its deepest dye,
From these, and different far in rich degrees,
Minds spring as various as the leaves of trees,
To follow taste and all her sweets explore
And Edens make, where deserts spread before.
In poesy's spells some all their raptures find
And revel in the melodies of mind.
There nature o'er the soul her beauty flings
In all the sweets and essences of things,
A face of beauty in a city crowd
Met, passed, and vanished like a summer cloud.
In poesy's vision more refined and fair
Taste reads o'erjoyed and greets her image there.
Dashes of sunshine and a page of may
Live there a whole life long one summer's day.
A blossom in its witchery of bloom
There gathered dwells in beauty and perfume;
The singing bird, the brook that laughs along,
There ceaseless sing and never thirsts for song.
A pleasing image to its page conferred
In living character and breathing word
Becomes a landscape heard and felt and seen,
Sunshine and shade one harmonizing green
Where meads and brooks and forests basking lie,
Lasting as truth and the eternal sky.

Thus truth to nature as the true sublime
Stands a mount Atlas overpeering time,
Styles may with fashions vary, tawdry, chaste,
Have had their votaries which each fancied taste.
From Donne's old homely gold, whose broken feet
Jostles the reader's patience from its seat,
To Pope's smooth rhymes that regularly play
In music's stated periods all the way,
That starts and closes, starts again and chimes
Its tuning gamut true as minster chimes.
From these old fashions stranger metres flow,
Half prose, half verse that stagger as they go;
One line starts smooth and then for room perplext
Elbows along and knocks against the next,
And half its neighbour, where a pause marks time,
There the clause ends : what follows is for rhyme.
Yet truth to nature will in all remain
As grass in winter glorifies the plain,
And over fashion's foils rise proud and high
As light's bright fountain in a cloudy sky.
The man of science in discovery's moods
Roams o'er the furze-clad heath's leaf-buried woods,
And by the simple brook in rapture finds
Treasures that wake the laugh of vulgar hinds,
Who see no further in his dark employs
Than village childern seeking after toys.
Then clownish hearts and ever heedless eyes
Find nought in nature they as wealth can prize;
With them self-interest and the thoughts of gain
Are nature's beauties : all beside are vain.
But he the man of science and of taste
Sees wealth far richer in the worthless waste
Where bits of lichen and a sprig of moss
Will all the raptures of his mind engross,
And bright-winged insects on the flowers of May
Shine pearls too wealthy to be cast away.

His joys run riot 'mid each juicy blade
Of grass where insects revel in the shade,
And minds of different moods will oft condemn
His taste as cruel: such the deeds to them
While he unconscious gibbets butterflies
And strangles beetles all to make us wise.
Tastes rainbow vision's own unnumbered hues
And every shade its sense of taste pursues.
The heedless mind may laugh, the clown may stare,
They own no soul to look for pleasure there.
Their grosser feelings in a coarser dress
Mock at the wisdom which they can't possess.
Some in recordless rapture love to breathe
Nature's wild Eden wood and field and heath,
In common blades of grass his thoughts will raise
A world of beauty to admire and praise,
Until his heart o'erflows with swarms of thought
To that great Being who raised life from nought.
The common weed adds graces to his mind
And gleams in beauty few beside may find,
Associations sweet each object breeds
And fine ideas upon fancy feeds.
He loves not flowers because they shed perfumes,
Or butterflies alone for painted plumes
Or birds for singing, although sweet it be,
But he doth love the wild and meadow lea,
There hath the flower its dwelling place and there
The butterfly goes dancing through the air.
He loves each desolate neglected spot
That seems in labour's hurry left forgot,
The warped and punished trunk of stunted oak
Freed from its bonds but by the thunder stroke,
As crampt by straggling ribs of ivy sere:
There the glad bird makes home for half the year.
But take these several beings from their homes,
Each beauteous thing a withered thought becomes;

Association fades, and, like a dream,
They are but shadows of the things they seem.
Torn from their homes and happiness they stand
The poor dull captives of a foreign land.
Some spruce and delicate ideas feed,
With them disorder is an ugly weed
And wood and heath a wilderness of thorns
No gardener sheers nor fashions nor adorns.
No spots give pleasure so forlorn and bare
But gravel walks would work rich wonders there.
With such wild natures beauty's run to waste
And art's strong impulse mars the truth of taste.
Such are the various moods that taste displays
Surrounding wisdom in concentring rays
Where threads of light from one bright focus run
As day's proud halo circles round the sun.

THE PROGRESS OF RHYME

O SOUL-ENCHANTING poesy,
Thou'st long been all the world with me;
When poor, thy presence grows my wealth,
When sick, thy visions give me health,
When sad, thy sunny smile is joy
And was from e'en a tiny boy.
When trouble was and toiling care
Seemed almost more than I could bear,
While threshing in the dirty barn
Or squashing in the ditch to earn
A pittance that would scarce allow
One joy to smooth my sweating brow
Where drop by drop would chase and fall,
Thy presence triumphed over all:
The vulgar they might frown and sneer,
Insult was mean but never near.

'Twas poesy's self that stopt the sigh
And malice met with no reply.
So was it in my earlier day
When sheep to corn had strayed away
Or horses closen gaps had broke,
Ere sun's head peeped or I awoke
My master's frowns might force the tear
But poesy came to check and cheer.
It glistened in my shamed eye
But ere it fell the woof was by.
I thought of luck in future days
When even he might find a praise.
I looked on poesy like a friend
To cheer me till my life should end.
'Twas like a parent's first regard
And love when beauty's voice was heard,
'Twas joy, 'twas hope, and maybe fear,
But still 'twas rapture everywhere.
My heart were it unmoved to dwell,
Nor care for one I loved so well
Through rough and smooth, through good and ill,
That led me and attends me still?
It was an early joy to me
That joy was love and poesy,
And but for thee my idle lay
Had ne'er been urged in early day,
The harp's imagination strung
Had ne'er been dreamed of but among
The flowers in summer's fields of joy
I'd lain an idle rustic boy,
No hope to think of fear or care
And even love a stranger there.
But poesy that vision flung
Around me as I hummed and sung,
I glowered on beauty passing by
Yet hardly turned my sheepish eye;

I worshipped, yet could hardly dare
Go show I knew the goddess there,
Lest my presumptuous stare should gain
But frowns, ill humour, and disdain.
My first ambition was its praise,
My struggles; ay, in early days
Had I by vulgar boldness torn
That hope when it was newly born,
By rudeness, gibes, and vulgar tongue
The curse of the unfeeling throng,
Their scorn had frowned upon the lay
And hope and song had died away.
And I with nothing to atone
Had felt myself indeed alone
But promises of days to come.
The very fields would seem to hum
Those burning days when I should dare
To sing aloud my worship there,
When beauty's self might turn its eye
Of praise: what could I do but try?
'Twas winter then, but summer shone
From heaven when I was all alone,
And summer came and every weed
Of great or little had its meed,
Without its leaves there wa'n't a bower
Nor one poor weed without its flower.
'Twas love and pleasure all along
I felt that I'd a right to song
And sung—but in a timid strain
Of fondness for my native plain;
For everything I felt a love,
The weeds below, the birds above;
And weeds that bloomed in summer's hours
I thought they should be reckoned flowers;
They made a garden free for all,
And so I loved them great and small,

And sung of some that pleased my eye,
Nor could I pass the thistle by,
But paused and thought it could not be
A weed in nature's poesy.
No matter for protecting wall,
No matter though they chance to fall
Where sheep and cows and oxen lie,
The kindly rain when they're adry
Falls on them with as plenteous showers
As when it waters garden flowers;
They look up with a blushing eye
Upon a tender watching sky,
And still enjoy the kindling smile
Of sunshine though they live with toil,
As garden flowers with all their care,
For nature's love is ever there.
And so it cheered me while I lay
Among their beautiful array
To think that I in humble dress
Might have a right to happiness
And sing as well as greater men;
And then I strung the lyre again
And heartened up o'er toil and fear
And lived with rapture everywhere,
Till dayshine to my themes did come.
Just as a blossom bursts to bloom
And finds itself in thorny ways,
So did my musings meet with praise,
And though no garden care had I
My heart had love for poesy,
A simple love, a wild esteem,
As heartfelt as the linnet's dream
That mutters in its sleep at night
Some notes from extasy's delight.
Thus did I dream o'er joys and lie
Muttering dream songs of poesy.

The night dislimned and waking day
Shook from wood leaves the drops away;
Hope came, storms calmed, and hue and cry
With her false pictures herded by,
With tales of help when help was not,
Of friends who urged to write or blot,
Whose taste were such that mine were shame
Had they not helped it into fame.
Poh! let the idle rumour ill,
Their vanity is never still;
My harp though simple was my own.
When I was in the fields alone
With none to help and none to hear
To bid me either hope or fear,
The bud or bee its chords would sound,
The air hummed melodies around,
I caught with eager ear the strain
And sung the music o'er again,
Or love or instinct flowing strong,
Fields were the essence of the song.
And fields and woods are still as mine,
Real teachers that are all divine,
So if my song be weak or lame
'Tis I, not they, who bear the blame,
But hope and cheer through good and ill,
They are my aids to worship still,
Still growing on a gentle tide
Nor foes could mar nor friends could guide;
Like pasture brooks through sun and shade,
Crooked as channels chance hath made,
It rambles as it loves to stray
And hope and feeling lead the way.
—Ay, birds, no matter what the tune
Or 'croak' or 'tweet', 'twas nature's boon
That brought them joy, and music flung
Its spell o'er every matin sung,

And e'en the sparrow's chirp to me
Was song in its felicity
When grief hung o'er me like a cloud
Till hope seemed even in her shroud.
I whispered poesy's spell till they
Gleamed round me like a summer's day;
When tempests o'er my labours sung
My soul to its responses rung,
And joined the chorus till the storm
Fell all unheeded, void of harm,
And each old leaning shielding tree
Were princely palaces to me,
Where I could sit me down and chime
My unheard rhapsodies to rhyme.
All I beheld of grand, with time
Grew up to beautiful sublime.
The arching groves of ancient limes
That into roofs like churches climbs,
Grain intertwisting into grain,
That stops the sun and stops the rain
And spreads a gloom that never smiles,
Like ancient halls and minster aisles,
While all without a beauteous screen
Of summer's luscious leaves is seen,
While heard that everlasting hum
Of insects haunting where they bloom,
As though 'twas nature's very place
Of worship, where her mighty race
Of insect life and spirits too
In summer time were wont to go,
Both insects and the breath of flowers,
To sing their maker's mighty powers.
I've thought so as I used to rove
Through Burghley Park, that darksome grove
Of limes where twilight lingered grey
Like evening in the midst of day.

I felt without a single skill
That instinct that would not be still,
To think of song sublime beneath
That heaved my bosom like my breath,
That burned and chilled and went and came
Without or uttering or a name,
Until the vision waked with time
And left me itching after rhyme.
Where little pictures idly tells
Of nature's powers and nature's spells,
I felt and shunned the idle vein,
Laid down the pen and toiled again,
But spite of all through good and ill
It was and is my worship still.
No matter how the world approved,
'Twas nature listened, I that loved;
No matter how the lyre was strung,
From my own heart the music sprung.
The cowboy with his oaten straw,
Although he hardly heard or saw
No more of music than he made,
'Twas sweet; and when I pluckt the blade
Of grass upon the woodland hill
To mock the birds with artless skill,
No music in the world beside
Seemed half so sweet, till mine was tried.
So my boy-worship poesy
Made e'en the muses pleased with me,
Until I even danced for joy,
A happy and a lonely boy,
Each object to my ear and eye
Made paradise of poesy.
I heard the blackbird in the dell
Sing sweet; could I but sing as well,
I thought, until the bird in glee
Seemed pleased and paused to answer me.

CLARE   K

And nightingales, O I have stood
Beside the jungle and the wood,
And o'er the old oak railing hung
To listen every note they sung,
And left boys making taws of clay
To muse and listen half the day.
The more I listened and the more
Each note seemed sweeter than before,
And aye so different was the strain
She'd scarce repeat the note again:
—'Chew-chew chew-chew,' and higher still:
'Cheer-cheer cheer-cheer,' more loud and shrill:
'Cheer-up cheer-up cheer-up,' and dropt
Low: 'tweet tweet jug jug jug,' and stopt
One moment just to drink the sound
Her music made, and then a round
Of stranger witching notes was heard:
'Wew-wew wew-wew, chur-chur chur-chur,
Woo-it woo-it': could this be her?
'Tee-rew tee-rew tee-rew tee-rew,
Chew-rit chew-rit,' and ever new,
'Will-will will-will, grig-grig grig-grig.'
The boy stopt sudden on the brig
To hear the 'tweet tweet tweet' so shrill,
The 'jug jug jug,' and all was still
A minute, when a wilder strain
Made boys and woods to pause again;
Words were not left to hum the spell.
Could they be birds that sung so well?
I thought, and maybe more than I,
That music's self had left the sky
To cheer me with its magic strain
And then I hummed the words again,
Till fancy pictured, standing by
My heart's companion poesy.
No friends had I to guide or aid

The struggles young ambition made.
In silent shame the harp was tried
And rapture's griefs the tune applied,
Yet o'er the songs my parents sung
My ear in silent musings hung.
Their kindness wishes did regard,
They sung, and joy was my reward.
All else was but a proud decree,
The right of bards and nought to me,
A title that I dared not claim
And hid it like a private shame.
I whispered aye and felt a fear
To speak aloud though none was near,
I dreaded laughter more than blame,
I dared not sing aloud for shame,
So all unheeded, lone and free,
I felt it happiness to be
Unknown, obscure, and like a tree
In woodland peace and privacy.
No, not a friend on earth had I
But my own kin and poesy,
Nor wealth, and yet I felt indeed
As rich as any body need
To be, for health and hope and joy
Was mine, although a lonely boy,
And what I felt, as now I sing,
Made friends of all and every thing
Save man the vulgar and the low,
The polished 'twas not mine to know
Who paid me in my after days
And gave me even more than praise:
'Twas then I found that friends indeed
Were needed when I'd less to need.
The pea that independent springs
When in its blossom trails and clings
To every help that lingers by,

K 2

And I when classed with poesy,
Who stood unburnt the heaviest shower,
Felt feeble as that very flower
And helpless all, but beauty's smile
Is harvest for the hardest toil,
Whose smiles I little thought to win
With ragged coat and downy chin,
A clownish silent aguish boy
Who even felt ashamed of joy,
So dirty, ragged, and so low,
With nought to recommend or show
That I was worthy e'en a smile.
Had I but felt amid my toil
That I in days to come should be
A little light in minstrelsy,
And in the blush of after days
Win beauty's smile and beauty's praise,
My heart with lovely fancy warm
Had even bursted with the charm,
And one, ay, one whose very name
I loved, whose look was even fame,
From rich delicious eyes of blue
In smiles and rapture ever new,
Her timid step, her fairy form,
Her face with blushes ever warm,
Praise did my rhyming feelings move:
I saw the blush and thought it love.
And all ambitious thee to please
My heart was ever ill at ease;
I saw thy beauty grow with days,
And tried song-pictures in thy praise,
And all of fair or beautiful
Were thine akin, nor could I pull
The blossoms that I thought divine
As hurting beauty like to thine.
So where they grew I let them be,

And though I dare not talk to thee
Of love, to them I talked aloud,
And grew ambitious from the crowd
With hopes that I one day should be
Beloved with the praise of thee.
But I mistook in early day
The world, and so our hopes decay.
Yet that same cheer in after toils
Was poesy, and still she smiles
As sweet as blossoms to the tree,
And hope, love, joy, are poesy.

PLEASURES OF FANCY

A PATH, old tree, goes by thee crooking on,
And through this little gate that claps and bangs
Against thy rifted trunk, what steps hath gone!
Though but a lonely way, yet mystery hangs
O'er crowds of pastoral scenes recordless here.
The boy might climb the nest in thy young boughs
That's slept half an eternity; in fear
The herdsman may have left his startled cows
For shelter when heaven's thunder voice was near;
Here too the woodman on his wallet laid
For pillow may have slept an hour away;
And poet pastoral, lover of the shade,
Here sat and mused half some long summer day
While some old shepherd listened to the lay.

TO CHARLES LAMB ON HIS ESSAYS

ELIA, thy reveries and visioned themes
To Care's lorn heart a luscious pleasure proves,
Wild as the mystery of delightful dreams,
Soft as the anguish of remembered loves;
Like records of past days their memory dances
'Mid the cool feelings manhood's reason brings,
As the unearthly visions of romances
Peopled with sweet and uncreated things,
And yet thy themes thy gentle worth enhances;
Then wake again thy wild harp's tenderest strings,
Sing on, sweet bard, let fairy loves again
Smile in thy dreams with angel extasies;
Bright o'er our minds will break the witching
    strain
Through the dull gloom of earth's realities.

SWORDY WELL

WE loved thee, Swordy Well, and love thee still.
Long was I with thee, tending sheep and cow,
In boyhood ramping up each steepy hill
To play at 'roly poly' down; and now,
A man, I trifle on thee, cares to kill,
Haunting thy mossy steeps to botanize
And hunt the orchis tribes where nature's skill
Doth like my thoughts run into phantasies,
Spider and bee all mimicking at will,
Displaying powers that fool the proudly wise,
Showing the wonders of great nature's plan
In trifles insignificant and small,
Puzzling the power of that great trifle man
Who finds no reason to be proud at all.

THE INSTINCT OF HOPE

Is there another world for this frail dust
To warm with life and be itself again?
Something about me daily speaks there must,
And why should instinct nourish hopes in vain?
'Tis nature's prophesy that such will be,
And everything seems struggling to explain
The close sealed volume of its mystery.
Time wandering onward keeps its usual pace
As seeming anxious of eternity,
To meet that calm and find a resting place.
E'en the small violet feels a future power
And waits each year renewing blooms to bring,
And surely man is no inferior flower
To die unworthy of a second spring?

PROVIDENCE

Some talk of providence with heedless tongue
That leads to riches and not happiness,
Which is but a new tune for fortune's song,
And one contentment cares not to profess.
It knows her seldom and it shuns her long,
And that kind providence least understood
Hath been my friend that helps me bear with wrong
And learns me out of evil to find good;
To hearten up against the heartless creeds
Of selfish interests leading blindly on,
To make one's poor faith wither 'mid the weeds
Of earth's deceptions; yet when these are gone
A voice within tells peace our one true friend:
And this is providence right worthy to commend.

FLATTERY

Go, flattery, go, thou nothing clothed in sound,
The voice of ages lives not on thy tongue,
Time treads thee like a shadow on the ground
As nothing-where and laugheth at the wrong.
Thou ten day's wonder of an idle noise,
Cease teasing truth with subtleties and lies;
Truth that thy every spider web destroys
With higher aim bids upward thoughts arise,
Where past the storm of strife the sickly praise,
The barefaced lie, in secret hatched and bred,
Is left unto the storm of after days,
And thy gay fluttering streets untenanted
Of friendships, age-swept, silent and alone,
Buried and chilled like cities into stone.

NATURE

How many pages of sweet nature's book
Hath poesy doubled down as favoured things,
Such as the wood-leaves in disorder shook
By startled stockdoves' hasty clapping wings,
Or green woodpecker that soft tapping clings
To grey oak trunks, till, scared by passing clown,
It bounces forth in airy ups and downs
To seek fresh solitudes; the circling rings
The idle puddock makes around the towns,
Watching young chickens by each cottage pen:
And such are each day's parti-coloured skies,
And such the landscape's charms o'er field and fen,
That meet the poet's never weary eyes
And are too many to be told again.

HOME PICTURES IN MAY

THE sunshine bathes in clouds of many hues
And morning's feet are gemmed with early dews,
Warm daffodils about the garden beds
Peep through their pale slim leaves their golden
    heads,
Sweet earthly nuns of Spring; the gosling broods
In coats of sunny green about the road
Waddle in extasy; and in rich moods
The old hen leads her flickering chicks abroad,
Oft scuttling 'neath her wings to see the kite
Hang wavering o'er them in the spring's blue light.
The sparrows round their new nests chirp with glee
And sweet the robin Spring's young luxury shares
Tootling its song in feathery gooseberry tree
While watching worms the gardener's spade unbares.

SUMMER EVENING

THE frog half fearful jumps across the path,
And little mouse that leaves its hole at eve
Nimbles with timid dread beneath the swath;
My rustling steps awhile their joys deceive,
Till past, and then the cricket sings more strong,
And grasshoppers in merry moods still wear
The short night weary with their fretting song.
Up from behind the molehill jumps the hare,
Cheat of his chosen bed, and from the bank
The yellowhammer flutters in short fears
From off its nest hid in the grasses rank,
And drops again when no more noise it hears.
Thus nature's human link and endless thrall,
Proud man, still seems the enemy of all.

AUTUMN

Me it delights in mellow autumn tide
To mark the pleasaunce that my eye surrounds,
The forest trees like coloured posies pied,
The uplands mealy grey and russet grounds;
Seeking for joy where joyaunce most abounds,
Not found, I ween, in courts and halls of pride,
Where folly feeds on flattery's sights and sounds,
And with sick heart but seemeth to be merry.
True pleasaunce is with humble food supplied,
Like shepherd swain who plucks the bramble berry
With savoury appetite from hedgerow briars,
Then drops content by molehill's sunny side,
Proving thereby low joys and small desires
Are easiest fed and soonest satisfied.

EMMONSAIL'S HEATH IN WINTER

I love to see the old heath's withered brake
Mingle its crimpled leaves with furze and ling,
While the old heron from the lonely lake
Starts slow and flaps his melancholy wing,
And oddling crow in idle motions swing
On the half rotten ashtree's topmost twig,
Beside whose trunk the gipsy makes his bed.
Up flies the bouncing woodcock from the brig
Where a black quagmire quakes beneath the tread,
The fieldfares chatter in the whistling thorn
And for the ewe round fields and clover rove,
And coy bumbarrels twenty in a drove
Flit down the hedgerows in the frozen plain
And hang on little twigs and start again.

GREENSWARD

Rich healthiness hedges the summer grass
Of each old close, and everywhere instills
Gladness to travellers while they pause and pass
The narrow pathway through the old molehills
Of glad neglected pastures; and I've thought
While sitting down upon their quiet laps
That no delight that rich men ever bought
Could equal mine, where quiet came unsought
While the cow mused beside the broken gaps
At the rich hay-close sweeping to the wind.
And as to pleasure, nature's gifts not few
Come to the heart as unto grass the dew,
For e'en her meanest gifts where'er we find
Are worth a praise as music to the mind.

THE WHEAT RIPENING

What time the wheat-field tinges rusty brown
And barley bleaches in its mellow grey
'Tis sweet some smooth mown baulk to wander down
Or cross the fields on footpath's narrow way
Just in the mealy light of waking day.
As glittering dewdrops moist the maiden's gown
And sparkling bounces from her nimble feet
Journeying to milking from the neighbouring town,
Making life light with song; and it is sweet
To mark the grazing herds and list the clown
Urge on his ploughing team with cheering calls,
And merry shepherds whistling toils begun,
And hoarse tongued bird-boy whose unceasing calls
Join the lark's ditty to the rising sun.

THE MEADOW HAY

I OFTEN roam a minute from the path
Just to luxuriate on the new mown swath
And stretch me at my idle length along,
Hum louder o'er some melody or song
While passing stranger slackens in his pace
And turns to wonder what can haunt the place,
Unthinking that an idle rhymster lies
Buried in the sweet grass and feeding phantasies.
This happy spirit of the joyous day
Stirs every pulse of life into the play
Of buoyant joy and extasy: I walk
And hear the very weeds to sing and talk
Of their delights as the delighted wind
Toys with them like play-fellows ever kind.

THE SALLOW

PENDANT o'er rude old ponds, or leaning o'er
The woodland's mossy rails, the sallows now
Put on their golden liveries, and restore
The Spring to splendid memories, ere a bough
Of whitethorn shows a leaf to say 'tis come;
And through the leafless underwood rich stains
Of sunny gold show where the sallows bloom,
Like sunshine in dark places, and gold veins
Mapping the russet landscape into smiles
At Spring's approach; nor hath the sallow palms
A peer for richness: ploughmen in their toils
Will crop a branch, smit with its golden charms,
While at its root the primrose' brimming eye
Smiles in his face and blooms delicious by.

THE FIRETAIL'S NEST

'TWEET' pipes the robin as the cat creeps by
Her nestling young that in the elderns lie,
And then the bluecap tootles in its glee,
Picking the flies from orchard apple tree,
And 'pink' the chaffinch cries its well known strain,
Urging its kind to utter 'pink' again,
While in a quiet mood hedgesparrows try
An inward stir of shadowed melody.
Around the rotten tree the firetail mourns
As the old hedger to his toil returns,
Chopping the grain to stop the gap close by
The hole where her blue eggs in safety lie.
Of everything that stirs she dreameth wrong
And pipes her 'tweet tut' fears the whole day long.

THE FEAR OF FLOWERS

THE nodding oxeye bends before the wind,
The woodbine quakes lest boys their flowers should
      find,
And prickly dogrose spite of its array
Can't dare the blossom-seeking hand away,
While thistles wear their heavy knobs of bloom
Proud as a warhorse wears its haughty plume,
And by the roadside danger's self defies;
On commons where pined sheep and oxen lie
In ruddy pomp and ever thronging mood
It stands and spreads like danger in a wood,
And in the village street where meanest weeds
Can't stand untouched to fill their husks with seed,
The haughty thistle o'er all danger towers,
In every place the very wasp of flowers.

WILD BEES

THESE children of the sun which summer brings
As pastoral minstrels in her merry train
Pipe rustic ballads upon busy wings
And glad the cotters' quiet toils again.
The white nosed bee that bores its little hole
In mortared walls and pipes its symphonies,
And never absent couzen, black as coal,
That Indian-like bepaints its little thighs,
With white and red bedight for holiday,
Right earlily a-morn do pipe and play
And with their legs stroke slumbers from their eyes.
And aye so fond they of their singing seem
That in their holes abed at close of day
They still keep piping in their honey dreams,
And larger ones that thrum on ruder pipe
Round the sweet smelling closen and rich woods
Where tawny white and red flushed clover buds
Shine bonnily and bean fields blossom ripe,
Shed dainty perfumes and give honey food
To these sweet poets of the summer field,
Me much delighting as I stroll along
The narrow path that hay laid meadow yields,
Catching the windings of their wandering song.
The black and yellow bumble first on wing
To buzz among the sallow's early flowers,
Hiding its nest in holes from fickle Spring
Who stints his rambles with her frequent showers;
And one that may for wiser piper pass,
In livery dress half sables and half red,
Who laps a moss ball in the meadow grass
And hoards her stores when April showers have fled;
And russet commoner who knows the face
Of every blossom that the meadow brings,

Starting the traveller to a quicker pace
By threatening round his head in many rings:
These sweeten summer in their happy glee
By giving for her honey melody.

TO CONTENT

CHEERFUL Content, thy home be mine,
Do not my suit disdain;
They who prefer the world's to thine
Shall find it false and vain;
From broken hopes and storms I fly
To hide me in thy peaceful sky.

The flatterers meet with smiles,
The cunning find their friends;
Whoso without makes pilgrimage
Shall meet but small amends;
As children they who in the sun
Seek flowers in winter and find none.

Some cringe to menial slaves,
Some worship haughty power,
Some bend the knee to knaves,
The price of earthly dower,
Which they who were not taught to pay
May see and empty turn away.

Earth's pleasure is to flatter,
Life's love is but to hate,
To praise what they in heart abuse,
Alas, in church and state,
And whoso makes not this their game
Shall keep their wants and shun the shame.

Thus flattery findeth friends
In every grade and state,
Thus telling truth offends
The lowly and the great,
Yet truth at last shall bloom and rise
When flattery's folly fades and dies.

Pride's pomps are shadows all,
Mere wealth is honour's toys,
Whose merits oft are small,
Whose praise but empty noise;
Rainbows upon the skies of May
Fade soon, but scarce so soon as they.

Then, sweet Content, thy home be mine;
If sorrows should pursue,
Thou'lt shake them from those smiles of thine
As morning does the dew,
And as thought's broken hopes decay
My heart shall struggle and be gay.

As hopes from earth shall disappear
With thee I'll not despair,
For thou canst look at heaven and hear
The vagrant calling there,
And see her smile and sweetly see
The loss she met was gain to me.

POEMS IN THE MANNER OF OLDER POETS

FAREWELL AND DEFIANCE TO LOVE

Love and thy vain employs, away
From this too oft deluded breast!
No longer will I court thy stay,
To be my bosom's teasing guest.
Thou treacherous medicine, reckon'd pure,
Thou quackery of the harass'd heart,
That kills what it pretends to cure,
    Life's mountebank thou art,

With nostrums vain of boasted powers,
That, ta'en, a worse disorder leave;
An asp hid in a group of flowers,
That bites and stings when few perceive;
Thou mock-peace to the troubled mind,
Leading it more in sorrow's way,
Freedom that leaves us more confined,
    I bid thee hence away.

Dost taunt, and deem thy power beyond
The resolution reason gave?
Tut! Falsity hath snapt each bond,
That kept me once thy quiet slave,
And made thy snare a spider's thread,
Which e'en my breath can break in twain;
Nor will I be, like Sampson, led
    To trust thy wiles again.

CLARE   L

Tempt me no more with rosy cheeks,
Nor daze my reason with bright eyes;
I'm wearied with thy wayward freaks,
And sicken at such vanities:
Be roses fine as e'er they will,
They, with the meanest, fade and die,
And eyes, tho' thick with darts to kill,
    Share all mortalities.

Feed the young bard, who madly sips
His nectar-draughts from folly's flowers,
Bright eyes, fair cheeks, and ruby lips,
Till music melts to honey showers;
Lure him to thrum thy empty lays,
While flattery listens to the chimes,
Till words themselves grow sick with praise
    And stop for want of rhymes.

Let such be still thy paramours,
And chaunt love's old and idle tune,
Robbing the spring of all its flowers,
And heaven of all her stars and moon,
To gild with dazzling similes
Blind folly's vain and empty lay:
I'm sober'd from such phantasies,
    So get thee hence away,

Nor bid me sigh for mine own cost,
Nor count its loss, for mine annoy,
Nor say my stubbornness hath lost
A paradise of dainty joy:
I'll not believe thee, till I know
That reason turns thy pampered ape,
And acts thy harlequin, to show
    That care's in every shape.

Heart-achings, sighs, and grief-wrung tears,
Shame-blushes at betrayed distress,
Dissembled smiles, and jealous fears,
Are aught but real happiness:
Then will I mourn what now I brave,
And suffer Celia's quirks to be
(Like a poor fate-bewilder'd slave,)
  The rulers of my destiny.

I'll weep and sigh whene'er she wills
To frown, and when she deigns to smile
It will be cure for all my ills,
And, foolish still, I'll laugh the while;
But till that comes, I'll bless the rules
Experience taught, and deem it wise
To hold thee as the game of fools,
  And all thy tricks despise.

TO JOHN MILTON

'FROM HIS HONOURED FRIEND, WILLIAM DAVENANT.'

Poet of mighty power, I fain
Would court the muse that honoured thee,
And, like Elisha's spirit, gain
  A part of thy intensity;
And share the mantle which she flung
Around thee, when thy lyre was strung.

Though faction's scorn at first did shun,
With coldness, thy inspired song,
Though clouds of malice pass'd thy sun,
  They could not hide it long;
Its brightness soon exhaled away
Dank night, and gained eternal day.

The critics' wrath did darkly frown
Upon thy muse's mighty lay;
But blasts that break the blossom down
    Do only stir the bay;
And thine shall flourish, green and long,
With the eternity of song.

Thy genius saw, in quiet mood,
Gilt fashion's follies pass thee by,
And, like the monarch of the wood,
    Tower'd o'er it to the sky,
Where thou couldst sing of other spheres,
And feel the fame of future years.

Though bitter sneers and stinging scorns
Did throng the muse's dangerous way,
Thy powers were past such little thorns,
    They gave thee no dismay;
The scoffer's insult pass'd thee by,
Thou smild'st and mad'st him no reply.

Envy will gnaw its heart away
To see thy genius gather root;
And as its flowers their sweets display
    Scorn's malice shall be mute;
Hornets that summer warmed to fly,
Shall at the death of summer die.

Though friendly praise hath but its hour,
And little praise with thee hath been;
The bay may lose its summer flower,
    But still its leaves are green;
And thine, whose buds are on the shoot,
Shall only fade to change to fruit.

Fame lives not in the breath of words,
In public praises' hue and cry;
The music of these summer birds
    Is silent in a winter sky,
When thine shall live and flourish on,
O'er wrecks where crowds of fames are gone.

The ivy shuns the city wall,
When busy-clamorous crowds intrude,
And climbs the desolated hall
    In silent solitude;
The time-worn arch, the fallen dome,
Are roots for its eternal home.

The bard his glory ne'er receives
Where summer's common flowers are seen,
But winter finds it when she leaves
    The laurel only green;
And time from that eternal tree,
Shall weave a wreath to honour thee.

A sunny wreath for poet's meed,
From Helicon's immortal soil,
Where sacred Time with pilgrim feet
    Walks forth to worship, not to spoil,
A wreath which Fame creates and bears,
And deathless genius only heirs.

Nought but thy ashes shall expire;
Thy genius, at thy obsequies,
Shall kindle up its living fire
    And light the muse's skies;
Ay, it shall rise, and shine, and be
A sun in song's posterity.

THE VANITIES OF LIFE

'Vanity of vanities, all is vanity.'—Solomon.

WHAT are life's joys and gains?
What pleasures crowd its ways,
That man should take such pains
To seek them all his days?
Sift this untoward strife
On which the mind is bent:
See if this chaff of life
Is worth the trouble spent.

Is pride thy heart's desire?
Is power thy climbing aim?
Is love thy folly's fire?
Is wealth thy restless game?
Pride, power, love, wealth, and all
Time's touchstone shall destroy,
And, like base coin, prove all
Vain substitutes for joy.

Dost think that pride exalts
Thyself in other's eyes,
And hides thy folly's faults,
Which reason will despise?
Dost strut, and turn, and stride,
Like walking weathercocks?
The shadow by thy side
Becomes thy ape, and mocks.

Dost think that power's disguise
Can make thee mighty seem?
It may in folly's eyes,
But not in worth's esteem,
When all that thou canst ask,
And all that she can give,
Is but a paltry mask
Which tyrants wear and live.

Go, let thy fancies range
And ramble where they may;
View power in every change,
And what is the display?
—The country magistrate,
The lowest shade in power,
To rulers of the state,
The meteors of an hour.

View all, and mark the end
Of every proud extreme,
Where flattery turns a friend,
And counterfeits esteem;
Where worth is aped in show,
That doth her name purloin,
Like toys of golden glow
That's sold for copper coin.

Ambition's haughty nod
With fancies may deceive,
Nay, tell thee thou'rt a god,
And wilt thou such believe?
Go, bid the seas be dry;
Go, hold earth like a ball,
Or throw thy fancies by,
For God can do it all.

Dost thou possess the dower
Of laws to spare or kill?
Call it not heavenly power
When but a tyrant's will.
Think what a God will do,
And know thyself a fool,
Nor, tyrant-like, pursue
Where He alone should rule.

Dost think, when wealth is won,
Thy heart has its desire?
Hold ice up to the sun,
And wax before the fire;
Nor triumph o'er the reign
Which they so soon resign;
In this world's ways they gain,
Insurance safe as thine.

Dost think life's peace secure
In houses and in land?
Go, read the fairy lure
To twist a cord in sand;
Lodge stones upon the sky,
Hold water in a sieve,
Nor give such tales the lie,
And still thine own believe.

Whoso with riches deals,
And thinks peace bought and sold,
Will find them slipping eels,
That slide the firmest hold:
Though sweet as sleep with health
Thy lulling luck may be,
Pride may o'erstride thy wealth,
And check prosperity.

Dost think that beauty's power
Life sweetest pleasure gives?
Go, pluck the summer flower,
And see how long it lives:
Behold, the rays glide on
Along the summer plain
Ere thou canst say they're gone,
And measure beauty's reign.

Look on the brightest eye,
Nor teach it to be proud;
View next the clearest sky,
And thou shalt find a cloud;
Nor call each face ye meet
An angel's, 'cause it's fair,
But look beneath your feet,
And think of what they are.

Who thinks that love doth live
In beauty's tempting show,
Shall find his hopes ungive,
And melt in reason's thaw.
Who thinks that pleasure lies
In every fairy bower,
Shall oft, to his surprise,
Find poison in the flower.

Dost lawless passions grasp?
Judge not thou deal'st in joy:
Its flowers but hide the asp,
Thy revels to destroy.
Who trusts a harlot's smile,
And by her wiles are led,
Plays, with a sword the while
Hung dropping o'er his head.

Dost doubt my warning song?
Then doubt the sun gives light,
Doubt truth to teach the wrong,
And wrong alone as right;
And live as lives the knave,
Intrigue's deceiving guest;
Be tyrant, or be slave,
As suits thy ends the best.

Or pause amid thy toils
For visions won and lost,
And count the fancied spoils,
If e'er they quit the cost:
And if they still possess
Thy mind, as worthy things,
Plat straws with bedlam Bess,
And call them diamond rings.

Thy folly's past advice,
Thy heart's already won,
Thy fall's above all price,
So go, and be undone;
For all who thus prefer
The seeming great for small
Shall make wine vinegar,
And sweetest honey gall.

Would'st heed the truths I sing,
To profit wherewithal,
Clip folly's wanton wing,
And keep her within call.
I've little else to give,
What thou canst easy try;
The lesson how to live
Is but to learn to die.

POEM ON DEATH

WHY should man's high aspiring mind
Burn in him with so proud a breath,
When all his haughty views can find
    In this world yields to Death?
The fair, the brave, the vain, the wise,
The rich, the poor, and great, and small,
Are each but worm's anatomies
    To strew his quiet hall.

Power may make many earthly gods,
Where gold and bribery's guilt prevails,
But Death's unwelcome, honest odds
  Kick o'er the unequal scales.
The flatter'd great may clamours raise
Of power, and their own weakness hide,
But Death shall find unlooked-for ways
  To end the farce of pride.

An arrow hurtel'd e'er so high,
From e'en a giant's sinewy strength,
In Time's untraced eternity
  Goes but a pigmy length;
Nay, whirring from the tortured string,
With all its pomp of hurried flight,
'Tis by the skylark's little wing
  Outmeasured in its height.

Just so man's boasted strength and power
Shall fade before Death's lightest stroke,
Laid lower than the meanest flower,
  Whose pride o'er-topt the oak;
And he who, like a blighting blast,
Dispeopled worlds with war's alarms
Shall be himself destroyed at last
  By poor despised worms.

Tyrants in vain their powers secure,
And awe slaves' murmurs with a frown,
For unawed Death at last is sure
  To sap the Babels down.
A stone thrown upward to the skye
Will quickly meet the ground agen;
So men-gods of earth's vanity
  Shall drop at last to men;

And Power and Pomp their all resign,
Blood-purchased thrones and banquet halls.
Fate waits to sack Ambition's shrine
     As bare as prison walls,
Where the poor suffering wretch bows down
To laws a lawless power hath passed;
And pride, and power, and king, and clown
     Shall be Death's slaves at last.

Time, the prime minister of Death!
There's nought can bribe his honest will.
He stops the richest tyrant's breath
     And lays his mischief still.
Each wicked scheme for power all stops,
With grandeurs false and mock display,
As eve's shades from high mountain tops
     Fade with the rest away.

Death levels all things in his march;
Nought can resist his mighty strength;
The palace proud, triumphal arch,
     Shall mete its shadow's length.
The rich, the poor, one common bed
Shall find in the unhonoured grave,
Where weeds shall crown alike the head
     Of tyrant and of slave.

ASYLUM POEMS

LEFT ALONE

LEFT in the world alone,
Where nothing seems my own,
And everything is weariness to me,
'Tis a life without an end,
'Tis a world without a friend,
And everything is sorrowful I see.

There's the crow upon the stack,
And other birds all black,
While bleak November's frowning wearily;
And the black cloud's dropping rain,
Till the floods hide half the plain,
And everything is dreariness to me.

The sun shines wan and pale,
Chill blows the northern gale,
And odd leaves shake and quiver on the tree,
While I am left alone,
Chilled as a mossy stone,
And all the world is frowning over me.

MY EARLY HOME

HERE sparrows build upon the trees,
And stockdove hides her nest;
The leaves are winnowed by the breeze
Into a calmer rest;
The black-cap's song was very sweet,
That used the rose to kiss;
It made the Paradise complete:
My early home was this.

The red-breast from the sweetbriar bush
       Dropt down to pick the worm;
On the horse-chestnut sang the thrush,
       O'er the house where I was born;
The moonlight, like a shower of pearls,
       Fell o'er this 'bower of bliss',
And on the bench sat boys and girls:
       My early home was this.

The old house stooped just like a cave,
       Thatched o'er with mosses green;
Winter around the walls would rave,
       But all was calm within;
The trees are here all green agen,
       Here bees the flowers still kiss,
But flowers and trees seemed sweeter then:
       My early home was this.

HOME YEARNINGS

O FOR that sweet, untroubled rest
       That poets oft have sung!—
The babe upon its mother's breast,
       The bird upon its young,
The heart asleep without a pain—
When shall I know that sleep again?

When shall I be as I have been
       Upon my mother's breast
Sweet Nature's garb of verdant green
       To woo to perfect rest—
Love in the meadow, field, and glen,
And in my native wilds again?

The sheep within the fallow field,
   The herd upon the green,
The larks that in the thistle shield,
   And pipe from morn to e'en—
O for the pasture, fields, and fen!
When shall I see such rest again?

I love the weeds along the fen,
   More sweet than garden flowers,
For freedom haunts the humble glen
   That blest my happiest hours.
Here prison injures health and me:
I love sweet freedom and the free.

The crows upon the swelling hills,
   The cows upon the lea,
Sheep feeding by the pasture rills,
   Are ever dear to me,
Because sweet freedom is their mate,
While I am lone and desolate.

I loved the winds when I was young,
   When life was dear to me;
I loved the song which Nature sung,
   Endearing liberty;
I loved the wood, the vale, the stream,
For there my boyhood used to dream.

There even toil itself was play;
   'Twas pleasure e'en to weep;
'Twas joy to think of dreams by day,
   The beautiful of sleep.
When shall I see the wood and plain,
And dream those happy dreams again?

MARY BATEMAN

My love she wears a cotton plaid,
　A bonnet of the straw;
Her cheeks are leaves of roses spread,
　Her lips are like the haw.
In truth she is as sweet a maid
　As true love ever saw.

Her curls are ever in my eyes,
　As nets by Cupid flung;
Her voice will oft my sleep surprise,
　More sweet than ballad sung.
O Mary Bateman's curling hair!
　I wake, and there is nothing there.

I wake, and fall asleep again,
　The same delights in visions rise;
There's nothing can appear more plain
　Than those rose cheeks and those bright eyes.
I wake again, and all alone
　Sits Darkness on his ebon throne.

All silent runs the silver Trent,
　The cobweb veils are all wet through,
A silver bead's on every bent,
　On every leaf a bleb of dew.
I sighed, the moon it shone so clear:
　Was Mary Bateman walking here?

MARY

The skylark mounts up with the morn,
The valleys are green with the Spring,
The linnets sit in the whitethorn,
To build mossy dwellings and sing;

I see the thornbush getting green,
I see the woods dance in the Spring,
But Mary can never be seen,
Though the all-cheering Spring doth begin.

I see the grey bark of the oak
Look bright through the underwood now;
To the plough plodding horses they yoke,
But Mary is not with her cow.
The birds almost whistle her name:
Say, where can my Mary be gone?
The Spring brightly shines, and 'tis shame
That she should be absent alone.

The cowslips are out on the grass,
Increasing like crowds at a fair;
The river runs smoothly as glass,
And the barges float heavily there;
The milkmaid she sings to her cow,
But Mary is not to be seen;
Can Nature such absence allow
At milking on pasture and green?

When Sabbath-day comes to the green.
The maidens are there in their best,
But Mary is not to be seen,
Though I walk till the sun's in the west.
I fancy still each wood and plain,
Where I and my Mary have strayed,
When I was a young country swain,
And she was the happiest maid.

But woods they are all lonely now,
And the wild flowers blow all unseen;
The birds sing alone on the bough,
Where Mary and I once have been.

CLARE   M

But for months she now keeps away,
And I am a sad lonely hind;
Trees tell me so day after day,
As slowly they wave in the wind.

Birds tell me, while swaying the bough,
That I am all threadbare and old;
The very sun looks on me now
As one dead, forgotten, and cold.
Once I'd a place where I could rest,
And love, for then I was free;
That place was my Mary's dear breast
And hope was still left unto me.

THE TELL-TALE FLOWERS

AND has the Spring's all glorious eye
    No lesson to the mind?
The birds that cleave the golden sky,
    Things to the earth resigned,
Wild flowers that dance to every wind,
Do they no memory leave behind?

Aye, flowers! The very name of flowers,
    That bloom in wood and glen,
Brings Spring to me in Winter's hours,
    And childhood's dreams again.
The primrose on the woodland lea
Was more than gold and lands to me.

The violets by the woodland side
    Are thick as they could thrive;
I 've talked to them with childish pride
    As things that were alive:
I find them now in my distress,
They seem as sweet, yet valueless.

The cowslips on the meadow lea,
  How have I run for them!
I looked with wild and childish glee
  Upon each golden gem:
And when they bowed their heads so shy
I laughed, and thought they danced for joy.

And when a man, in early years,
  How sweet they used to come,
And give me tales of smiles and tears,
  And thoughts more dear than home:
Secrets which words would then reprove,
They told the names of early love.

The primrose turned a babbling flower
  Within its sweet recess:
I blushed to see its secret bower,
  And turned her name to bless.
The violets said the eyes were blue:
I loved, and did they tell me true?

The cowslips, blooming everywhere,
  My heart's own thoughts could steal:
I nipt them that they should not hear:
  They smiled, and would reveal;
And o'er each meadow, right or wrong,
They sing the name I've worshipped long.

The brook that mirrored clear the sky,
  Full well I know the spot;
The mouse-ear looked with bright blue eye,
  And said 'Forget-me-not'.
And from the brook I turned away,
But heard it many an after day.

The king-cup on its slender stalk,
      Within the pasture dell,
Would picture there a pleasant walk
      With one I loved so well.
It said 'How sweet at eventide
'Twould be, with true love at thy side.'

And on the pasture's woody knoll
      I saw the wild bluebell,
On Sundays where I used to stroll
      With her I loved so well:
She culled the flowers the year before;
These bowed, and told the story o'er.

And every flower that had a name
      Would tell me who was fair;
But those without, as strangers, came
      And blossomed silent there:
I stood to hear, but all alone:
They bloomed and kept their thoughts unknown.

But seasons now have nought to say,
      The flowers no news to bring:
Alone I live from day to day,
      Flowers deck the bier of Spring;
And birds upon the bush or tree
All sing a different tale to me.

I'LL DREAM UPON THE DAYS TO COME

I'LL lay me down on the green sward,
Mid yellowcups and speedwell blue,
And pay the world no more regard,
But be to Nature leal and true.
Who break the peace of hapless man
But they who Truth and Nature wrong?
I'll hear no more of evil's plan,
But live with Nature and her song.

Where Nature's lights and shades are green,
Where Nature's place is strewn with flowers,
Where strife and care are never seen,
There I'll retire to happy hours,
And stretch my body on the green,
And sleep among the flowers in bloom,
By eyes of malice seldom seen,
And dream upon the days to come.

I'll lay me by the forest green,
I'll lay me on the pleasant grass;
My life shall pass away unseen;
I'll be no more the man I was.
The tawny bee upon the flower,
The butterfly upon the leaf,
Like them I'll live my happy hour,
A life of sunshine, bright and brief.

In greenwood hedges, close at hand,
Build, brood, and sing the little birds,
The happiest things in the green land,
While sweetly feed the lowing herds,
While softly bleat the roving sheep.
Upon the green grass will I lie,
A Summer's day, to think and sleep,
Or see the clouds sail down the sky.

BIRDS, WHY ARE YE SILENT?

WHY are ye silent,
  Birds? Where do ye fly?
Winter's not violent,
  With such a Spring sky.
The wheatlands are green, snow and frost are away;
Birds, why are ye silent on such a sweet day?

  By the slated pig-stye
    The redbreast scarce whispers:
  Where last Autumn's leaves lie
    The hedge sparrow just lispers.
And why are the chaffinch and bullfinch so still,
While the sulphur primroses bedeck the wood hill?

  The bright yellow-hammers
    Are strutting about,
  All still, and none stammers
    A single note out.
From the hedge starts the blackbird, at brook
  side to drink:
I thought he'd have whistled but he only said 'prink'.

  The tree-creeper hustles
    Up fir's rusty bark;
  All silent he bustles;
    We needn't say hark.
There's no song in the forest, in field, or in wood,
Yet the sun gilds the grass as though come in
  for good.

  How bright the odd daisies
    Peep under the stubbs!
  How bright pilewort blazes
    Where ruddled sheep rubs
The old willow trunk by the side of the brook,
Where soon for blue violets the children will look!

By the cot green and mossy
　　Feed sparrow and hen:
On the ridge brown and glossy
　　They cluck now and then.
The wren cocks his tail o'er his back by the stye,
Where his green bottle nest will be made by and
　　bye.

Here's bunches of chickweed,
　　With small starry flowers,
Where red-caps oft pick seed
　　In hungry Spring hours.
And bluecap and blackcap, in glossy Spring coat,
Are a-peeping in buds without singing a note.

Why silent should birds be
　　And sunshine so warm?
Larks hide where the herds be
　　By cottage and farm.
If wild flowers were blooming and fully set in the
　　Spring
May-be all the birdies would cheerfully sing.

THE INVITATION

COME hither, my dear one, my choice one, and rare one,
　　And let us be walking the meadows so fair,
Where on pilewort and daisies the eye fondly gazes,
　　And the wind plays so sweet in thy bonny brown
　　hair.

Come with thy maiden eye, lay silks and satins by;
　　Come in thy russet or grey cotton gown;
Come to the meads, dear, where flags, sedge, and reeds
　　appear,
　　Rustling to soft winds and bowing low down.

Come with thy parted hair, bright eyes, and forehead
    bare;
  Come to the whitethorn that grows in the lane;
To banks of primroses, where sweetness reposes,
  Come, love, and let us be happy again.

Come where the violet flowers, come where the
    morning showers
  Pearl on the primrose and speedwell so blue;
Come to that clearest brook that ever runs round
    the nook
  Where you and I pledged our first love so true.

THE LOVER'S INVITATION

Now the wheat is in the ear, and the rose is on
    the brere,
And blue-caps so divinely blue, with poppies of
    bright scarlet hue,
Maiden, at the close o' eve, wilt thou, dear, thy
    cottage leave,
        And walk with one that loves thee?

When the even's tiny tears bead upon the grassy
    spears,
And the spider's lace is wet with its pinhead blebs
    of dew,
Wilt thou lay thy work aside and walk by brook-
    lets dim descried,
        Where I delight to love thee?

While thy footfall lightly press'd tramples by the sky-
    lark's nest,
And the cockle's streaky eyes mark the snug place
    where it lies,
Mary, put thy work away, and walk at dewy close o'day
        With me to kiss and love thee.

There's something in the time so sweet, when lovers
    in the evening meet,
The air so still, the sky so mild, like slumbers of
    the cradled child,
The moon looks over fields of love, among the ivy
    sleeps the dove;
        To see thee is to love thee.

THE MORNING WALK

THE linnet sat upon its nest,
By gales of morning softly prest,
His green wing and his greener breast
    Were damp with dews of morning:
The dog-rose near the oaktree grew,
Blush'd swelling 'neath a veil of dew,
A pink's nest to its prickles grew,
    Right early in the morning.

The sunshine glittered gold, the while
A country maiden clomb the stile;
Her straw hat couldn't hide the smile
    That blushed like early morning.
The lark, with feathers all wet through,
Looked up above the glassy dew,
And to the neighbouring corn-field flew,
    Fanning the gales of morning.

In every bush was heard a song,
On each grass blade, the whole way long,
A silver shining drop there hung,
    The milky dew of morning.
Where stepping-stones stride o'er the brook
The rosy maid I overtook.
How ruddy was her healthy look,
    So early in the morning!

I took her by the well-turned arm,
And led her over field and farm,
And kissed her tender cheek so warm,
    A rose in early morning.
The spiders' lace-work shone like glass,
Tied up to flowers and cat-tail grass;
The dew-drops bounced before the lass,
    Sprinkling the early morning.

Her dark curls fanned among the gales,
The skylark whistled o'er the vales,
I told her love's delightful tales
    Among the dews of morning.
She cropt a flower, shook off the dew,
And on her breast the wild rose grew;
She blushed as fair, as lovely, too,
    The living rose of morning.

THE MARCH NOSEGAY

THE bonny March morning is beaming
    In mingled crimson and grey,
White clouds are streaking and creaming
    The sky till the noon of the day;
The fir deal looks darker and greener,
    And grass hills below look the same;
The air all about is serener,
    The birds less familiar and tame.

Here's two or three flowers for my fair one,
    Wood primroses and celandine too;
I oft look about for a rare one
    To put in a posy for you.
The birds look so clean and so neat,
    Though there's scarcely a leaf on the grove;
The sun shines about me so sweet,
    I cannot help thinking of love.

So where the blue violets are peeping,
  By the warm sunny sides of the woods,
And the primrose, 'neath early morn weeping,
  Amid a large cluster of buds,
(The morning it was such a rare one,
  So dewy, so sunny, and fair,)
I sought the wild flowers for my fair one,
  To wreath in her glossy black hair.

BONNY MARY O!

THE morning opens fine, bonny Mary O!
The robin sings his song by the dairy O!
Where the little Jenny wrens cock their tails among
    the hens,
  Singing morning's happy songs with Mary O!

The swallow 's on the wing, bonny Mary O!
Where the rushes fringe the spring, bonny Mary O!
Where the cowslips do unfold, shaking tassels all
    of gold,
  Which make the milk so sweet, bonny Mary O!

There's the yellowhammer's nest, bonny Mary O!
Where she hides her golden breast, bonny
    Mary O!
On her mystic eggs she dwells, with strange writing
    on their shells,
  Hid in the mossy grass, bonny Mary O!

There the spotted cow gets food, bonny Mary O!
And chews her peaceful cud, bonny Mary O!
In the mole-hills and the bushes, and the clear brook
    fringed with rushes
  To fill the evening pail, bonny Mary O!

. . . . . .

Where the gnat swarms fall and rise under evening's
    mellow skies,
  And on flags sleep dragon flies, bonny Mary O!

  And I will meet thee there, bonny Mary O!
  When a-milking you repair, bonny Mary O!
And I'll kiss thee on the grass, my buxom, bonny lass,
  And be thine own for aye, bonny Mary O!

WHERE SHE TOLD HER LOVE

    I SAW her crop a rose
    Right early in the day,
    And I went to kiss the place
    Where she broke the rose away
    And I saw the patten rings
    Where she o'er the stile had gone,
    And I love all other things
    Her bright eyes look upon.
If she looks upon the hedge or up the leafing tree,
The whitethorn or the brown oak are made dearer
    things to me.

    I have a pleasant hill
    Which I sit upon for hours,
    Where she cropt some sprigs of thyme
    And other little flowers;
    And she muttered as she did it
    As does beauty in a dream,
    And I loved her when she hid it
    On her breast, so like to cream,
Near the brown mole on her neck that to me a
    diamond shone;
Then my eye was like to fire, and my heart was
    like to stone.

There is a small green place
Where cowslips early curled,
Which on Sabbath day I traced,
The dearest in the world.
A little oak spreads o'er it,
And throws a shadow round,
A green sward close before it,
The greenest ever found:
There is not a woodland nigh nor is there a green
    grove,
Yet stood the fair maid nigh me and told me all
    her love.

THE FACE I LOVE SO DEARLY

SWEET is the violet, scented pea,
Haunted by red-legged, sable bee,
But sweeter far than all to me
    Is she I love so dearly;
Than perfumed pea and sable bee,
    The face I love so dearly.

Sweeter than hedgerow violets blue,
Than apple blossoms' streaky hue,
Or black-eyed bean-flower blebbed with dew
    Is she I love so dearly;
Than apple flowers or violets blue
    Is she I love so dearly.

Than woodbine upon branches thin,
The clover flower, all sweets within,
Which pensive bees do gather in,
    Three times as sweet, or nearly,
Is the cheek, the eye, the lip, the chin
    Of her I love so dearly.

EVENING

In the meadow's silk grasses we see the black snail,
Creeping out at the close of the eve, sipping dew,
While even's one star glitters over the vale,
Like a lamp hung outside of that temple of blue.
I walk with my true love adown the green vale,
The light feathered grasses keep tapping her shoe;
In the whitethorn the nightingale sings her sweet tale,
And the blades of the grasses are sprinkled with dew.

If she stumbles I catch her and cling to her neck,
As the meadow-sweet kisses the blush of the rose:
Her whisper none hears, and the kisses I take
The mild voice of even will never disclose.
Her hair hung in ringlets adown her sweet cheek,
That blushed like the rose in the hedge hung with dew;
Her whisper was fragrance, her face was so meek,
The dove was the type on't that from the bush flew.

EVENING

'Tis evening; the black snail has got on his track,
    And gone to its nest is the wren,
And the packman snail, too, with his home on his
        back,
    Clings to the bowed bents like a wen.

The shepherd has made a rude mark with his foot
    Where his shadow reached when he first came,
And it just touched the tree where his secret love cut
    Two letters that stand for love's name.

The evening comes in with the wishes of love,
    And the shepherd he looks on the flowers,
And thinks who would praise the soft song of the
        dove,
    And meet joy in these dew-falling hours.

For Nature is love, and finds haunts for true love,
    Where nothing can hear or intrude;
It hides from the eagle and joins with the dove,
    In beautiful green solitude.

AUTUMN

I love the fitful gust that shakes
    The casement all the day,
And from the glossy elm tree takes
    The faded leaves away,
Twirling them by the window pane
With thousand others down the lane.

I love to see the shaking twig
    Dance till the shut of eve,
The sparrow on the cottage rig,
    Whose chirp would make believe
That Spring was just now flirting by
In Summer's lap with flowers to lie.

I love to see the cottage smoke
    Curl upwards through the trees,
The pigeons nestled round the cote
    On November days like these;
The cock upon the dunghill crowing,
The mill sails on the heath a-going.

The feather from the raven's breast
    Falls on the stubble lea,
The acorns near the old crow's nest
    Drop pattering down the tree;
The grunting pigs, that wait for all,
Scramble and hurry where they fall.

THE BEANFIELD

A BEANFIELD full in blossom smells as sweet
As Araby, or groves of orange flowers,
Black-eyed and white, and feathered to one's feet,
How sweet they smell in morning's dewy hours!
When seething night is left upon the flowers,
And when morn's sun shines brightly o'er the field,
The bean bloom glitters in the gems of showers,
And sweet the fragrance which the union yields
To battered footpaths crossing o'er the fields.

THE SWALLOW

SWIFT goes the sooty swallow o'er the heath,
Swifter than skims the cloud-rack of the skies;
As swiftly flies its shadow underneath,
And on his wing the twittering sunbeam lies,
As bright as water glitters in the eyes
Of those it passes; 'tis a pretty thing,
The ornament of meadows and clear skies:
With dingy breast and narrow pointed wing,
Its daily twittering is a song to Spring.

TO MY WIFE.—A VALENTINE.

O ONCE I had a true love,
    As blest as I could be:
Patty was my turtle dove,
    And Patty she loved me.
We walked the fields together,
    By roses and woodbine,
In Summer's sunshine weather,
    And Patty she was mine.

TO MY WIFE

We stopped to gather primroses,
    And violets white and blue,
In pastures and green closes
    All glistening with the dew.
We sat upon green mole-hills,
    Among the daisy flowers,
To hear the small birds' merry trills,
    And share the sunny hours.

The blackbird on her grassy nest
    We would not scare away,
Who nuzzling sat with brooding breast
    On her eggs for half the day.
The chaffinch chirruped on the thorn,
    And a pretty nest had she;
The magpie chattered all the morn
    From her perch upon the tree.

And I would go to Patty's cot,
    And Patty came to me;
Each knew the other's very thought
    Under the hawthorn tree.
And Patty had a kiss to give,
    And Patty had a smile,
To bid me hope and bid me love,
    At every stopping stile.

We loved one Summer quite away,
    And when another came,
The cowslip close and sunny day,
    It found us much the same.
We both looked on the selfsame thing,
    Till both became as one;
The birds did in the hedges sing,
    And happy time went on.

CLARE   N

The brambles from the hedge advance,
 In love with Patty's eyes:
On flowers, like ladies at a dance,
 Flew scores of butterflies.
I claimed a kiss at every stile,
 And had her kind replies.
The bees did round the woodbine toil,
 Where sweet the small wind sighs.

Then Patty was a slight young thing;
 Now she's long past her teens;
And we've been married many springs,
 And mixed in many scenes.
And I'll be true for Patty's sake,
 And she'll be true for mine;
And I this little ballad make,
 To be her valentine.

MAID OF THE WILDERNESS

MAID of the wilderness,
Sweet in thy rural dress,
Fond thy rich lips I press
 Under this tree.

Morning her health bestows,
Sprinkles dews on the rose,
That by the bramble grows:
 Maid happy be.
Womanhood round thee glows,
 Wander with me.

The restharrow blooming,
The sun just a-coming,
Grass and bushes illuming,
 And the spreading oak tree;

Come hither, sweet Nelly,

.   .   .   .   .   .

The morning is loosing
 Its incense for thee.
The pea-leaf has dews on;
 Love wander with me.

We'll walk by the river,
And love more than ever;
There's nought shall dissever
 My fondness from thee.

Soft ripples the water,
Flags rustle like laughter,
And fish follow after;
 Leaves drop from the tree.
Nelly, Beauty's own daughter,
 Love, wander with me.

BONNY LASSIE O!

O THE evening's for the fair, bonny lassie O!
To meet the cooler air and join an angel there,
 With the dark dishevelled hair,
  Bonny lassie O!

The bloom's on the brere, bonny lassie O!
Oak apples on the tree; and wilt thou gang to see
 The shed I've made for thee,
  Bonny lassie O!

'Tis agen the running brook, bonny lassie O!
In a grassy nook hard by, with a little patch of sky,
 And a bush to keep us dry,
  Bonny lassie O!

168   BONNY LASSIE O!

There's the daisy all the year, bonny lassie O!
There's the king-cup bright as gold, and the
        speedwell never cold,
    And the arum leaves unrolled,
            Bonny lassie O!

O meet me at the shed, bonny lassie O!
With the woodbine peeping in, and the roses like
        thy skin
    Blushing, thy praise to win,
            Bonny lassie O!

I will meet thee there at e'en, bonny lassie O!
When the bee sips in the bean, and grey willow
        branches lean,
    And the moonbeam looks between,
            Bonny lassie O!

YOUNG JENNY

The cockchafer hums down the rut-rifted lane
Where the wild roses hang and the woodbines entwine,
And the shrill squeaking bat makes his circles again
Round the side of the tavern close by the sign.
The sun is gone down like a wearisome queen,
In curtains the richest that ever were seen.

The dew falls on flowers in a mist of small rain,
And, beating the hedges, low fly the barn owls;
The moon with her horns is just peeping again,
And deep in the forest the dog-badger howls;
In best bib and tucker then wanders my Jane
By the side of the woodbines which grow in the lane.

On a sweet eventide I walk by her side;
In green hoods the daisies have shut up their eyes.
Young Jenny is handsome without any pride;
Her eyes (O how bright!) have the hue of the skies.
O 'tis pleasant to walk by the side of my Jane
At the close of the day, down the mossy green lane.

We stand by the brook, by the gate, and the stile,
While the even star hangs out his lamp in the sky;
And on her calm face dwells a sweet sunny smile,
While her soul fondly speaks through the light of
    her eye.
Sweet are the moments while waiting for Jane;
'Tis her footsteps I hear coming down the green
    lane.

ADIEU!

'ADIEU, my love, adieu!
Be constant and be true
As the daisies gemmed with dew,
        Bonny maid.'
The cows their thirst were slaking,
Trees the playful winds were shaking;
Sweet songs the birds were making
        In the shade.

The moss upon the tree
Was as green as green could be,
The clover on the lea
        Ruddy glowed;
Leaves were silver with the dew,
Where the tall sowthistles grew,
And I bade the maid adieu
        On the road.

Then I took myself to sea,
While the little chiming bee
Sung his ballad on the lea,
        Humming sweet;
And the red-winged butterfly
Was sailing through the sky,
Skimming up and bouncing by
        Near my feet.

I left the little birds,
And sweet lowing of the herds,
And couldn't find out words,
        Do you see,
To say to them good-bye,
Where the yellow cups do lie;
So heaving a deep sigh,
        Took to sea.

MY TRUE LOVE IS A SAILOR

'TWAS somewhere in the April time,
  Not long before the May,
A-sitting on a bank o' thyme
  I heard a maiden say,
' My true love is a sailor,
  And ere he went away
We spent a year together,
  And here my lover lay.

The gold furze was in blossom,
  So was the daisy too;
The dew-drops on the little flowers
  Were emeralds in hue.
On this same Summer morning,
  Though then the Sabbath day,
He cropt me Spring pol'ant'uses,
  Beneath the whitethorn may.

He cropt me Spring pol'ant'uses,
    And said if they would keep
They'd tell me of love's fantasies,
    For dews on them did weep.
And I did weep at parting,
    Which lasted all the week;
And when he turned for starting
    My full heart could not speak.

The same roots grow pol'ant'us' flowers
    Beneath the same haw-tree;
I cropt them in morn's dewy hours,
    And here love's offerings be.
O come to me my sailor beau
    And ease my aching breast;
The storms shall cease to rave and blow,
    And here thy life find rest.'

THE GIPSY LASS

JUST like the berry brown is my bonny lassie O!
And in the smoky camp lives my bonny lassie O!
    Where the scented woodbine weaves
    Round the white-thorn's glossy leaves:
The sweetest maid on earth is my gipsy lassie O!

The brook it runs so clear by my bonny lassie O!
And the blackbird singeth near my bonny lassie O!
    And there the wild briar rose
    Wrinkles the clear stream as it flows
By the smoky camp of my bonny lassie O!

The groundlark singeth high o'er my bonny lassie O!
The nightingale lives nigh my gipsy lassie O!
    They're with her all the year,
    By the brook that runs so clear,
And there's none in all the world like my gipsy
    lassie O!

With a bosom white as snow is my gipsy lassie O!
With a foot like to the roe is my bonny lassie O!
    Like the sweet birds she will sing,
    While echo it will ring:
Sure there's none in the world like my bonny
    lassie O!

CLOCK-A-CLAY

In the cowslip pips I lie,
Hidden from the buzzing fly,
While green grass beneath me lies,
Pearled with dew like fishes' eyes,
Here I lie, a clock-a-clay,
Waiting for the time o' day.

While the forest quakes surprise,
And the wild wind sobs and sighs,
My home rocks as like to fall,
On its pillar green and tall;
When the pattering rain drives by
Clock-a-clay keeps warm and dry.

Day by day and night by night,
All the week I hide from sight;
In the cowslip pips I lie,
In the rain still warm and dry;
Day and night, and night and day,
Red, black-spotted clock-a-clay.

My home shakes in wind and showers,
Pale green pillar topped with flowers,
Bending at the wild wind's breath,
Till I touch the grass beneath;
Here I live, lone clock-a-clay,
Watching for the time of day.

LITTLE TROTTY WAGTAIL

Little trotty wagtail he went in the rain,
And twittering, tottering sideways he ne'er got
    straight again.
He stooped to get a worm, and looked up to get a
    fly,
And then he flew away ere his feathers they were
    dry.

Little trotty wagtail, he waddled in the mud,
And left his little footmarks, trample where he would.
He waddled in the water-pudge, and waggle went
    his tail,
And chirrupt up his wings to dry upon the garden
    rail.

Little trotty wagtail, you nimble all about,
And in the dimpling water-pudge you waddle in and
    out;
Your home is nigh at hand, and in the warm pig-stye,
So, little Master Wagtail, I'll bid you a good-bye.

GRAVES OF INFANTS

Infants' gravemounds are steps of angels, where
Earth's brightest gems of innocence repose.
God is their parent, so they need no tear;
He takes them to his bosom from earth's woes,
A bud their lifetime and a flower their close.
Their spirits are the Iris of the skies,
Needing no prayers; a sunset's happy close.
Gone are the bright rays of their soft blue eyes;
Flowers weep in dew-drops o'er them, and the gale
    gently sighs.

Their lives were nothing but a sunny shower,
Melting on flowers as tears melt from the eye.
Each death   .   .   .   .
Was tolled on flowers as Summer gales went by.
They bowed and trembled, yet they heaved no sigh,
And the sun smiled to show the end was well.
Infants have nought to weep for ere they die;
All prayers are needless, beads they need not tell,
White flowers their mourners are, Nature their passing
    bell.

THE DYING CHILD

HE could not die when trees were green,
    For he loved the time too well.
His little hands, when flowers were seen,
    Were held for the bluebell,
        As he was carried o'er the green.

His eye glanced at the white-nosed bee;
    He knew those children of the Spring:
When he was well and on the lea
    He held one in his hands to sing,
        Which filled his heart with glee.

Infants, the children of the Spring!
    How can an infant die
When butterflies are on the wing,
    Green grass, and such a sky?
        How can they die at Spring?

He held his hands for daisies white,
    And then for violets blue,
And took them all to bed at night
    That in the green fields grew,
        As childhood's sweet delight.

And then he shut his little eyes,
    And flowers would notice not;
Birds' nests and eggs caused no surprise,
    He now no blossoms got:
        They met with plaintive sighs.

When Winter came and blasts did sigh,
    And bare were plain and tree,
As he for ease in bed did lie
    His soul seemed with the free,
        He died so quietly.

LOVE LIVES BEYOND THE TOMB

Love lives beyond the tomb,
And earth, which fades like dew!
    I love the fond,
The faithful, and the true.

Love lives in sleep:
'Tis happiness of healthy dreams:
    Eve's dews may weep,
But love delightful seems.

'Tis seen in flowers,
And in the morning's pearly dew;
    In earth's green hours,
And in the heaven's eternal blue.

'Tis heard in Spring
When light and sunbeams, warm and kind,
    On angel's wing
Bring love and music to the mind.

And where's the voice,
So young, so beautiful, and sweet
As Nature's choice,
Where Spring and lovers meet?

Love lives beyond the tomb,
And earth, which fades like dew!
I love the fond,
The faithful, and the true.

I AM!

I AM! yet what I am none cares or knows,
My friends forsake me like a memory lost;
I am the self-consumer of my woes,
They rise and vanish in oblivious host,
Like shades in love and death's oblivion lost;
And yet I am! and live with shadows tost

Into the nothingness of scorn and noise,
Into the living sea of waking dreams,
Where there is neither sense of life nor joys,
But the vast shipwreck of my life's esteems;
And e'en the dearest—that I loved the best—
Are strange—nay, rather stranger than the rest.

I long for scenes where man has never trod;
A place where woman never smil'd or wept;
There to abide with my creator, GOD,
And sleep as I in childhood sweetly slept:
Untroubling and untroubled where I lie;
The grass below—above the vaulted sky.

GLOSSARY

page

2   *Dithering*, shaking with cold.

8   *Lump away*, beat with a heavy sound.

9   *Chelp*, chirp.

9   *Taunts*, tosses.

10   *Swaliest*, coolest.

11   *The gad*, the gadfly.

11   *Drowking*, drooping.

11   *Teasel*, the fuller's thistle.

17   *Bleb*, bubble.

19   *Slive*, to do anything slyly.

20   *Morts*, great number.

21   *Come mull!* milkmaid's cry to her cow.

22   *Soodling*, sauntering.

29   *Whims*, probably *whins*, furze.

43   *Gleg*, glance.

45   *Stoven*, stump

48   *Chumbling*, gnawing.

56   *Twilly willy*, woollen gown.

72   *Elting*, moist, damp.

89   *Beesom*, furze.

89   *Ling*, heather.

92   *Stooks*, the sheaves of corn, set up together, and covered by two.

98   *Mouldiwarps*, moles.

DISTRIBUTORS
for the Wordsworth Poetry Library

AUSTRALIA, BRUNEI,
MALAYSIA & SINGAPORE

Reed Editions
22 Salmon Street
Port Melbourne
Vic 3207
Australia

Tel: (03) 646 6716
Fax: (03) 646 6925

GREAT BRITAIN & IRELAND

Wordsworth Editions Ltd
Cumberland House
Crib Street
Ware
Hertfordshire SG12 9ET

HOLLAND & BELGIUM

Uitgeverij en Boekhandel
Van Gennup BV, Spuistraat 283
1012 VR Amsterdam, Holland

INDIA

Om Book Service
1690 First Floor
Nai Sarak, Delhi - 110006

Tel: 3279823/3265303
Fax: 3278091

ITALY

Magis Books
Piazza della Vittoria 1/C
42100 Reggio Emilia

Tel: 0522-452303
Fax: 0522-452845

NEW ZEALAND

Whitcoulls Limited
Private Bag 92098, Auckland

SOUTHERN AFRICA

Struik Book Distributors (Pty) Ltd
Graph Avenue
Montague Gardens
7441
P O Box 193
Maitland
7405
South Africa

Tel: (021) 551-5900
Fax: (021) 551-1124

USA, CANADA & MEXICO

Universal Sales & Marketing
230 Fifth Avenue
Suite 1212
New York, NY 10001 USA

Tel: 212-481-3500
Fax: 212-481-3534